DICTIONARY OF
Oriental Rugs

with a monograph on
identification by weave

Ivan C. Neff & Carol V. Maggs

AD. DONKER / PUBLISHER

AD. DONKER LTD
29 King Street
London WC2E 8JD

AD. DONKER (PTY) LTD
Craighall Mews
Jan Smuts Avenue
Craighall Park
2196 Johannesburg

First published 1977

ISBN 0 949937 35 5

Design and layout by Jack Beaumont, Johannesburg
Typeset in VIP Palatino by Dieter Zimmermann (Pty) Ltd, Johannesburg
Reproduction by Unifoto (Pty) Ltd., Cape Town
Printed and bound by Creda Press (Pty) Ltd, Cape Town

'The lower part of his dress was
particularly improper, and he kept his
boots on in his room, without any
consideration for the carpet he was treading
upon, which struck me as a custom
subversive of all decorum.'

James Morier
The Adventures of Hajji Babu of Ispahan

To all those of similar sentiment who
respect and enjoy the remaining treasures
of one of the greatest folkcrafts the
world has ever known, we dedicate this work.

Ivan C. Neff and Carol V. Maggs

Contents

List of illustrations

Acknowledgements

We would like to express our gratitude to the people who have contributed to this work in many ways:

Rugs illustrated – W. A. C. Greatz, Henri Lidchi and Co. (Pty) Ltd, Museum of Fine Arts, Boston, Mass., Ami Negbi, J. W. Nel, Persian Carpet Gallery, T. O. Reimer, K. Scholtz, Walter Schwitter, F. C. Wilson.

Map – Dave Angus, Iain Connochi, John Earl.

Photography – Bert Blikslager, Richard Kirshner, the photographic department of the Museum of Fine Arts, Boston, Mass., Andre Strauss and Associates (Pty) Ltd, Adrianus van Helfteren.

Others have generously made available to us their knowledge, experience, skill and time, and some must be named as friends and mentors: Bert Blikslager, Pat Fiske, Alex Juran, Sybil Maggs, H. McCoy Jones, Ami Negbi, Larry Salmon, Walter Schwitter, George Seybolt.

We wish to thank the following for permission to quote from published works: Gerald Duckworth and Company Ltd (A. Cecil Edwards, *The Persian Carpet* and George W. O'Bannon, *The Turkoman Carpet*); J. B. Lippincott Company (Arthur U. Dilley, *Oriental Rugs and Carpets,* revised and enlarged by Maurice S. Dimand. Copyright 1931 by Charles Scribner's Sons, copyright renewed © 1959 by Arthur Urbane Dilley. Copyright © 1959 by Maurice S. Dimand); and Siawosch Azadi (*Turkoman Carpets*).

Meaning of rug names: an introduction

Expert dealers with decades of experience acquire a cognitive ability to identify rugs, an ability which, to the inexperienced, appears to be nothing more than sheer intuition. Their knowledge is built up by handling and studying hundreds of rugs of different types, origins and eras every year, and is sometimes described by that esoteric and frustrating term 'feel'. This term includes the tactile meaning of the word, but it also includes an understanding of the use of colour, the elements of the design, the way the ends are finished, the way the edges are made, the structure of the weave, and finally the overall appearance of all of those features taken together.

Some aspects of this expertise have been translated into literature that can be studied but the single most important feature of structure, namely, the appearance of the weave, has not. The preparation of this monograph was undertaken in an attempt to commence filling this gap. Our object is to persuade our readers that an illustration of the front of the rug does not tell the whole story. Nor is the addition of a technical analysis sufficient unless it is accompanied by an actual-size illustration of a section of the back of the rug. The point we emphasize throughout is that whatever learned conclusions are drawn concerning the origin of design features, these frequently have little relevance to the origin of a rug itself unless they are confirmed by the visible evidence disclosed by the weave as seen on the back of the rug.

Whilst preparing the monograph, it became clear that any assertive comments on the value of the weave as a means of identification would have to refer to all known rugs – but, known to whom, was the disheartening problem. The only way to resolve this was to compile a list of all names that have been used, and attempt to unravel their significance.

The dictionary includes over six hundred names. Not for one moment do we believe that this is all-inclusive; a few names used solely in academic circles have been left out and new names will arise from time to time. We have made every effort to compile a reference book that we hope will explain the reasons for some of the existing confusion in rug name usage.

Rug names are of several different kinds. Some, such as tribal names, refer to the people who made them, for example, Qashqa'i or Tekke. Others refer to the period in which they were made, and use the name of the reigning monarch or dynasty, such as Seljuk or Mughal. The great majority of names are those of towns, cities, districts and villages. In some cases, such as Kashan or Qum, the names indicate that the rugs were made in those places, and here it is usually manufactory work that is referred to. Often a town name will simply mean the marketing centre of an area where village or tribal rugs are produced. Samarkand and Shiraz are examples of this use. Other town or village names, particularly for modern rugs, are used by dealers to describe different qualities of work from the area around that town or village. Examples of this are the modern use of the names 'Arak', 'Sarouk' and 'Ahar'. And again, some town and village names have come to be used to differentiate between the various designs used in a particular area. Whether or not these designs were at one time the exclusive property of the villages whose names they bear, is no longer known. Ulrich Schürmann's (1965) classification of Caucasian rugs uses this method extensively. For example, the name 'Chondzoresk' is used to describe a design which is not the prerogative of one particular area as some of the rugs with this design are made in the Kazak technique, and others in the Karabagh technique. Some names refer to the method of weaving that was used, such as 'palas', 'soumak' and 'kelim' and by themselves do not indicate where or by whom the article was made. Another group of names found in the literature and in academic circles is used to describe a type which is often a subdivision of a larger group. These names such as 'Bragança', 'Sanguszko' and 'Nigde' are often taken from the name of the owner or the place where the type was first discovered. Also included in the dictionary are a number of Persian, Turkish, Turkoman and Armenian words which are used to describe bags and rugs of various shapes and sizes made to fulfil various functions.

Many rugs are described by more than one name, and some are given different names by different dealers. These names may, but do not necessarily, conflict, but may confuse the less informed person. For example, a rug of a certain shape may be called a 'juval' which is a Turkoman word for a large rectangular bag. The same piece might be described as a 'Pendeh', meaning that it was made near the Pendeh oasis. A third name for this piece might be 'Saryk' meaning that it was the work of the Saryk tribe of Turkoman. All three names are correct and in fact can be used in combination, as 'Pendeh Saryk juval', providing a more satisfactory description than any one of the three names on its own.

A number of names included in the dictionary are no longer used, but they are recorded because they are to be found in old texts, catalogues and inventories. Some new rug-names may well have been omitted. It is very likely that new names will appear as long as the rug knotting industry continues to exist.

A problem in producing the dictionary has been determining what spellings to adopt from the vast variety to be found in books, catalogues and advertisements. The policy followed has been to place in the most prominent position what has seemed to be the spelling most commonly used in literature and by the knowledgeable rug dealers. In brackets follow other spellings, not necessarily all the known forms; but an attempt has been made to include the most dissimilar ones as the differences are occasionally so great as to appear to be different names, and not just alternative spellings. Even this will not satisfy everyone as the transliteration of foreign names into English is not finally established. Names rendered into the various European languages can have very different spellings. Two examples are: *Awschan* (German) and *Afshan* (English); *Dshebrail* (German) and *Jabraeel* (English). When referring to places, both on the map and in the text, the spellings of the National Geographic Society of Washington, D.C. have been used with a few exceptions. In the case of the Turkish form 'Uşak', we believe that the nearest English transliteration is 'Ushak', and as this is also the most common spelling for the rug name, it seemed pedantic to use the two different spellings in the same sentence, one for the place and another for the rugs, so we have simply used the form 'Ushak'. The same applies to Mashhad and Meshed. The modern form 'Baluchi' has been used in all recent works when referring to these people and their rugs, but most dealers' catalogues still use the spelling 'Belouch' for the rugs. In this case we have used both spellings although it is a somewhat uncomfortable compromise.

In the explanation of each rug name, we have attempted to indicate in which way the rug is related to its name. This has a bearing on the conditions under which it was made, whether urban or rural; whether it was made in a manufactory or workshop as it is frequently called, or in a weaver's own home as a domestic activity. The manufactory rugs were more commercially orientated and the older ones more self-consciously works of art than the tribal rugs which were primarily made to serve a purpose in the life of the weaver. The difference between the attitudes of weavers living in urban and in rural tribal conditions is discussed more fully below.

The attempt to explain the meaning of rug names is in itself an exercise in the identification of rugs. In accordance with our theme, we have indicated where possible whether a rug has a distinctive weave structure, or whether it is a subdivision of a larger group. The Senneh rugs have a distinctive structure, whereas a rug such as a Kaputarahang has a structure the same as all rugs of the Hamadan group.

Sometimes, when dealing with names referred to in old texts but no longer used, neither approach is possible. In the absence of illustrations of the front and back of a rug it is often impossible to interpret what an author may be referring to. It also happens on occasions that two authors have used the same name to describe two very distinct types. In these instances we have endeavoured to deduce from the available evidence what was intended, but occasionally even that is impossible. As will be explained, some names were deliberately concocted as an expedient where definite attribution was unknown.

Every rug name has some reference, whether implied or explicit, to a place of origin, but that may be so wide an area as to include a number of distinct rug types. A feature that is stable and common to all rugs, wherever they were made, is therefore a necessary part of any attempted explanation of their names. The monograph explains why the weave is the most stable feature, common to all rugs, and therefore why it has been used in the dictionary as the main feature distinguishing one rug, or rug type, from another. For this reason the monograph and the dictionary are inseparable.

Weave pattern: a monograph

Concept of weave pattern

For about one hundred years Oriental rugs have been studied in the West, although they have been known and admired since at least the fourteenth century. These studies have attempted to discover how and when they were made, and to identify the people who made them. Rug knotting is often described as an Islamic art, and it is true that the great majority of surviving rugs were made during the Islamic era, in fact since the twelfth century. The best-known Persian designs are certainly of Islamic origin, such as the prayer rug whose 'mihrab' or 'prayer arch' is derived from Islamic mosque architecture. But we now know that the rug art goes back much further and was well known in Old Testament times and must pre-date even the Assyrians and Babylonians. Until 1949, the oldest-known fragments of piled rugs were those which had been discovered near Turfan in East Turkestan by Sir Aurel Stein. These were reckoned to date from between the third and sixth centuries A.D. In 1949, S.I. Rudenko, a Russian anthropologist, discovered the Pazyryk Carpet which dates from between the third and fifth centuries B.C., that is, between six hundred and eleven hundred years earlier than the Turfan fragments. Soon after this discovery, Rudenko unearthed another fragment of a knotted carpet at Bashadar some one hundred kilometres to the west of Pazyryk, and this fragment pre-dates the Pazyryk Carpet by at least one hundred years.

In the work of identifying the origin of the many different kinds of rugs, tremendous and painstaking effort has been applied to the study of their designs. The history of Oriental rug design is a fascinating and highly complex study. Much of the work that has been done on the subject has produced very interesting and valuable results. There has been an advance during this century in the understanding of the origins of certain designs and the influences that operated throughout the rug weaving world causing the dissemination and evolution of design motifs.

Although several authorities, particularly the earlier ones, have referred to the significance of the structure of rugs in regard to their provenance, this aspect has not been systematically studied as has that of design. This is not really surprising as all the beauty of colour and design is on the front of the rug, and a study of the back, on which the detail of the weaving technique can be seen, requires a drier, more academic approach.

In spite of the far greater interest of the design, colour and pile of rugs, almost everyone, when looking at rugs, will at some stage turn over a corner and examine the weave. This is done by expert and novice alike, in the first case by one who knows he will find certain information there, and in the second, by one who believes that the back is of importance, but does not quite know why.

The importance of the back of rugs lies in the fact that the weave is the single most reliable feature in identifying their provenance, or at least in grouping them into classes for the purpose of establishing their origin. Structural alikeness will help towards determining the place of origin or the people who made them with less fallibility than will design similarities. The tempting tendency to identify rugs according to their designs is unreliable and indeed, misleading. The word 'tempting' is used deliberately, as even distinguished authorities, aware though they are of the importance of the weave, are often distracted by the compelling nature of a rug's design, and fail to take note of the less exciting, but at the same time, more trustworthy, evidence of the weave on the back.

John Kimberly Mumford wrote the following in 1900, yet today the validity of his observations is still commonly overlooked: '... many patterns were so widely adopted that only by the character of the ground threads, oftentimes, could the fabric be identified as the product of any particular town or district' (p.84). A similar but more recent comment is to be found in a work by Andrei Andreyevich Bogolyubov; in the 'Editor's Introduction to the Plates', J.M.A. Thompson (1973) writes: 'Therefore by itself the gul is no guide to the tribal origin of a piece. The particular style of weaving, the traditional use of colour and fine ornamental details are a much more reliable guide . . .' (p.24).

Among the spate of authors who have followed Mumford, both scholars and rug dealers, many have referred to the fact that a study of weave or structure frequently provides an aid to identification, and sometimes the sole means of identification. In many books mention is made of structural features and one often reads such comments as, 'From the weaving technique it is apparent that this rug was made in Kashan.' Yet, for some unaccountable reason, neither museums nor authors have hitherto included photographic representations of the weave patterns of the rugs they illustrate. Although a few authors have shown one or two magnified pictures of weaves, magnification is unsuitable for the purpose of comparison and as an aid to identification, because it is what the eye sees that is important. The illustrations of the weaves included in this work are therefore all lifesize. True colour representation is also important to show coloured wefts where these are used.

Walter A. Hawley in 1913 was the first author to describe the characteristics of structure to be seen in various rugs. Unfortunately, a description does not provide a visual image of the distinctive features. For example, compare two of Hawley's descriptions: 'The rows of knots are firmly pressed down. *Warp*, cotton; each of the two threads encircled by a knot is equally prominent at back. *Weft*, generally cotton, frequently wool; of coarse diameter. A thread of weft crosses only once without slack between every two rows of knots, so that the white spots of transverse cotton warp exposed at the back have a quincunx appearance' (p. 124); and 'The rows of knots are closely pressed down, but the yarn of knots is not drawn tight against the warp. *Warp*, generally cotton, occasionally linen, rarely silk. Each of the two threads encircled by a knot is equally prominent at back. *Weft*, generally cotton, occasionally wool . . . A single thread of small diameter crosses only once between every two rows of

20

knots, so that the white spots of transverse warp exposed at back have a quincunx appearance' (p. 135).

These descriptions, though accurate, are practically identical and could well illustrate the same rug. And yet they refer to two very different weaves, namely, those of a Hamadan and a Senneh respectively. Plates 23 and 69 in this work will show how plain are the differences to the eye.

The colour plates included in this work show the complete rug as is usual in rug books. But, because of the emphasis which this work places on the visible differences in weaves, and because it is impossible to describe these differences adequately, each rug picture is accompanied by an actual-size reproduction of that portion of the back of the carpet which best illustrates the significant features of the weave.

Most authorities when dealing with the structural aspect of rugs will describe in considerable detail the direction of the twist of the warp, weft and pile yarns and their ply, and will mention which knot, the Senneh (asymmetrical or open), or Ghiordes (symmetrical or closed), was used. The analysis of these component features of structure is clearly essential to the proper description of a textile, but a technical analysis of this sort can amount to little more than a sterile academic exercise unless some conclusion is drawn from the analysis, which is seldom the case. It is not the object of this work to describe or analyse the structure and materials of rugs. A technical analysis does not show what the synthesis looks like. Under the subheading, 'Methodology of identification', we illustrate that the weaves of rugs with identical structural analyses may nevertheless be very different in appearance. Our purpose is therefore to show that the *visible* pattern formed on the back of a knotted rug is of the utmost importance. This 'weave pattern' as we call it, is often in fact, the hallmark or handwriting of a weaving group. It is the manual habit trained into the weavers from childhood which ultimately unmasks their identity. Their conscious effort goes into the execution of the design. The back of the rug is formed out of sight and simply as a result of this almost unconscious manual habit.

Because it is the visible pattern or final result of the structural technique that is being considered, the term 'weave pattern' has been adopted. The weave pattern is the pattern formed on the back of the rug by the interweaving of the warp and weft fibres, and includes the shape and angle of the knots, and their visible relationship to one another. Generally, the most singular feature of the weave pattern is the weft, how it is used, its colour and its form. Some aspects of the traditional methods of weaving which distinguish different types of rugs are the degree of depression of the alternate warp threads or the absence of such depression, and the peculiarity of the number of times the weft traverses the warp between the rows of knots. In the weavings of some types of rugs it invariably crosses only once, in some twice, and in others three or more times. These features are important constituents of weave pattern.

By concentrating on the term 'weave', the authors have deliberately used a narrower term than 'structure'. Weave might be said to be the major factor in structure, and it is here taken to exclude the other structural features of material, dye and length of pile, though these will be referred to at various times. When speaking of the Oriental rug in this text, it is always the knotted rug that is referred to.

Siawosch Azadi (1975) has made the following remark: 'Although technical analyses have been undertaken in as much detail as is possible, that is not to say that we have no more to learn on the subject; as yet we have neither sufficient material nor experience to be certain' (p. 4). Although we do not disagree with Azadi's last remark, if it is applied solely to ethnographic and historical data, we would rather suggest that what is lacking is a systematic collation of existing material, using weave pattern as the basic criterion and point of comparison. A technique similar to fingerprint identification could be readily adapted in simplified form for this type of study. It is interesting to note that rug dealers, who handle large numbers of rugs, are conscious of weave pattern when identifying rugs to a greater extent than museums and scholars, but naturally they are doing this for the purpose of their business and regrettably their experience has not been presented in illustrated form.

A problem exists in that rugs, carpets and other knotted weavings, are dispersed throughout the world, many being found in private collections in Western countries, while some valuable pieces are in Soviet museums. In neither of these situations are they very readily accessible. It would be an impossible task to bring them all together, and indeed this would be unnecessary. A close study of the colour plates in this book which show details of weave pattern will demonstrate, we believe, that a far more extensive use could be made of specialized photography, not only when describing textiles but also – and perhaps of even more importance – when comparing pieces which are housed far apart and cannot easily be brought together.

It is essential at this point to mention that the rugs illustrated were made largely in the nineteenth century, a few were made during this century, but weave pattern as a means of identification relates to rugs of all eras though it is less applicable to rugs of the twentieth century than to all earlier ones. Indeed, the further back one goes, the greater the validity of the argument. Modern rugs, on the other hand, are to some extent a different commodity, as there have been greater changes in the craft in the past fifty years than in the preceding several hundred years.

Problem of design
The history of our millennium in Central and western Asia is one of conquest by major empires – the Mongols, Persians, Turks and Russians – as they succeeded one another in power and territorial domination. During this period the nomadic peoples also engaged in inter-tribal and clan fighting for pastures and wells; in the Caucasus, the mountain people raided the valleys for livestock and crops. Throughout these tempestuous times trading influences were at work. Even though the Silk Road was closed for many centuries due to the hazards presented by wars and local strife, it was reopened in the late thirteenth century, and continued to exert its influence for hundreds of years. Then there were the localized caravan routes and the trade that was carried on in the villages and towns, including the great market centres such as Samarkand, Bokhara, Khiva, Herat, Tabriz and Istanbul. Contact between the different peoples varied in degree, but was often considerable. Market places provided a continuous exposure to designs from other regions and people. This inevitably led to copying and modification of design motifs.

When diverging from their own traditional designs, a group might simply adopt a design that appealed to them, but of far greater importance must have been the influence of the markets. Many people made woven goods for sale in addition to those they needed for themselves. We know that Turkish rugs were made for European markets as early as the sixteenth century and possibly earlier, and they were certainly known in Europe in the fourteenth century when they first appeared in Italian paintings. Designs which proved commercially successful became more widely used, in many cases resulting in the sacrifice of other, sometimes older, traditional designs.

An example of straightforward copying occurred in Turkey in the nineteenth century when, because of the high prices paid for Ghiordes and Kula rugs, the village of Panderma started to copy Ghiordes and Kula designs. For some reason the beautiful native rugs of Panderma were less popular or less well known. At some stage the practice of false 'antiquing' of these copies of Ghiordes rugs arose, but a study of their weave pattern will expose the fakes.

The question of copying or borrowing of designs is even more complex than this. There are many instances of weavers being moved to a new area usually to set up a manufactory. Kerman and Tabriz weavers were taken at different times to Turkey for this purpose, and Persian weavers were brought in to establish the craft in India by the Mughal Emperor Akbar (1556-1605), who was descended from the Mongol Tamerlane. Persian designs were used in the new weaving centres, but gradually these were modifed, and a local design character developed.

Another divergence from traditional design motifs is to be found among the Turkoman. It is believed that to varying degrees the rug design motifs of the Central Asian Turkoman tribes had in the past a significance beyond that of pure design. Totemism, as a remnant of the shamanistic religion of pre-Islamic times, survived until fairly recently, as did other aspects of shamanism, and it is possible that at some time there was a link between the tribes' onghuns (totems) and the design motifs of their rugs. It is also possible that the different guls (major design motifs) were originally related to tamghas (cattle-brands) and therefore, when the Saryk and the Tekke conquered a large part of the Salor,

24

they took over the cattle-brands and also the guls of their vanquished enemies. It is doubtful that the relationship of guls and tamghas can be traced back from the rugs we know now, though there is reason to believe that the bird motifs which appear in many of the tribal designs represent onghuns. These totems were all, as far as we know, birds of prey, among the Turkoman tribes.

In spite of the changes that must have taken place in tribal designs, it is clear that the tribal and nomadic peoples adhered to their design characteristics to a far greater extent, and for much longer, than did the village or townspeople who more readily borrowed designs.

Azadi (1975) discusses the ethnographic significance of both the primary and secondary ornaments in Turkoman weavings. With the assistance of the scholarly work of Professor Moschkova on Turkoman design motifs, Azadi shows how complex the whole picture of tribal designs had become by the end of the nineteenth century. We tend to assume that in the centuries before the Turkoman hordes became trapped between the advancing Persians and Russians, the tribal motifs were more clearly differentiated. We will probably never know whether this is true or not. Great significance was attached by Moschkova to the way in which minor ornamentation was used, and there is no doubt that, based on studies that have been done, it is fairly simple to identify the typical products of the major Turkoman groups from the design motifs alone. It is also true, however, that a large number of very good old Turkoman rugs are not typical examples of the work of one of these groups. Many show a mixture of design characteristics or atypical colouring, and it would really be guesswork to decide which design features are the significant ones when attempting to determine which tribe produced the piece. This admixture of design features became more and more common from the late nineteenth century, and frequently poses problems to the design devotees who are hard-pressed to find a satisfactory label for rugs of this kind.

One of the strongest motives for warfare between the Turkoman tribes and their neighbours was the possession of the oases, and sections of almost all the major groups – the Salor, Tekke, Saryk, Yomut and Ersari – were settled at one time or another in, or near, the oases of Merv and Pendeh in southern Turkestan. Here there was a considerable amount of contact between the tribes, and borrowing of designs took place. It appears that the oasis dwellers were more market-conscious than the nomads or, at least, being close to the market place, were more accessible to the demands of the merchants. At any rate, the 'hybrid' Turkoman rugs, those that show mixed design, colour or structural features, were often made near oases, those of Merv and Pendeh being very much cases in point.

Examples of Turkoman rugs dating from the end of the nineteenth century show many instances of design borrowing which we believe were motivated more by commercial popularity than any other factor. We refer in particular to the frequent use of the Salor gul in rugs produced by the Tekke and Saryk and less frequently by other tribes. The weave pattern of these pieces will almost always indicate whether or not they were made by the Salor. We say 'almost always', because there is still some confusion and doubt as to what the true Salor weave pattern looks like, a point we discuss more fully in the dictionary.

Carpets have been an object of commerce throughout the rug knotting world for a very long time and it has even been suggested by scholars that the Pazyryk Carpet, made between the third and fifth centuries B.C., was an object of commerce, and had been made on commission, possibly for a Scythian chieftain. Trade in rugs has taken place at all social levels, from the village market up to the commissioning of great carpets by nobles, sultans and shahs. This has meant that fashion and the taste of the buyer have influenced the designs and colours used by weavers. This influence was felt to the greatest extent in the towns, and to the least extent, and much later, by the remote nomadic tribes. From the early nineteenth century onwards, the European taste for French designs led to carpets being commissioned by the powerful Russian families in Georgia, to be woven in the Caucasus in Aubusson and Savonnerie designs or modifications of them. Such designs were also used in the Persian weaving centres such as Kerman, Senneh and Bijar for rugs destined for the eastern and western European countries. This point will be referred to again below, but for the moment, it suffices to show that it is just one of the many cases, and far more could be cited, of the borrowing and copying of Oriental as well as European designs. So widespread was this practice that it would have made the determining of rug provenance almost impossible if there were no other means of doing so.

Differences in weave pattern

It follows in all of the instances mentioned above, that to know the source of the *design* of a rug is not at all the same thing as identifying the place where the rug was made, or the people who made it. The only way the correct parentage of these rugs can be established is by reference to the weave pattern and materials used. It really is a remarkable fact that, in spite of national and tribal wars, migrations and commercial interaction, methods of rug construction used by different groups changed relatively little over long periods of time.

The differences in the weave patterns of the various types of rug are often easily recognized, but sometimes they are so subtle that they will not be apparent to anybody who has not paid considerable attention to them. They exist, however, and have existed for many generations. This may seem surprising when one considers the simplicity of the craft, and even more surprising that such basically simple techniques do result in at least sixty identifiable differences and can result in far more, as Dilley (1959) pointed out: 'In reality, there is a possible total of some ten thousand different effects, as a little computation will prove. The number of warp to the inch commonly varies from eight to forty, making a possible difference of thirty-two. The position of warp may be flat, double or intermediate; total difference, three. The number of weft to the inch varies from four to forty, making a possible difference of thirty-six. The position of weft, depending on tension, is straight, circular and semi-circular; total difference, three. Actually, there are not ten thousand or even one thousand variations in the surfaces of the backs; and of whatever number there is, the "rug man" uses for identification only a few dozen' (p. 264).

At this point, the reader is referred to the following plates as an illustration of how different the weave patterns evolved by various groups of people can look:

| Ersari Afghan | (Plate 15) | Yürük | (Plate 81) |
| Tekke | (Plate 75) | Senneh | (Plate 69) |

Sarouk (old)   (Plate 63)   Kirshehir   (Plate 41)

The Yürük and Kirshehir are Anatolian, the Sarouk and Senneh are Persian, and the Tekke and Ersari Afghan are Turkoman. Among this group of rugs is an example of a weave pattern that is known to have remained the same for well over two hundred years, namely, the Senneh. The example is by no means unique, but it is nonetheless remarkable when one considers that the rugs were made in north-western Iran surrounded on all sides by weaving influences of different identity, none of which have affected the technique which is peculiar to the village of Senneh, or Sanandaj as it is now known. Even more remarkable is the fact that the Senneh weavers, who are Kurds, developed a technique that is not remotely similar to any other Kurdish weave. Even the feel of the back of a Senneh is peculiar to these rugs. The feel is granular and so pronounced that, except where the back is badly worn, identification by feel alone is quite possible.

In an attempt to explain the constancy of weave patterns, one looks for an answer in the way of life and social forms of the weaving peoples. In pre-industrial Central and western Asia, people's lives were confined very largely to the town, village, rural area or tribe of their birth. There were few travellers apart from the merchants. The movement of the nomads was of a different order. It was not, like the merchants, to make contact with other people, but to find pastures for their flocks on which their survival and freedom depended. Their wandering life tended to isolate them from other people with whom their contacts, where they were not openly hostile, were generally transient and therefore superficial. For all these people, the identity of the town, village or nomadic group was of far greater significance than it would be nowadays. Another factor which reinforced the inward-looking nature of these communities was that many of them were formed of tribal groups, such as the Bakhtiari, the Kurds, the Qashqa'i, for all of whom tribal loyalty and cohesion was a far stronger reality than loyalty to a nation which was either non-existent or at best a very vague concept.

Each of these smaller social groups, whether tribal or not, constituted a very close and enduring community. It could be said that as these self-contained local groups had their own dialect, so the weavers had their own local technique, which was different from, though related to, that of their neighbours. Contact with other groups of people in the market place could and did have the effect of influencing the designs used by different groups, especially when it was apparent that the merchants preferred certain kinds of designs to others. But this type of contact was insufficient to affect the weaving technique used in the production of these designs.

If one accepts that distinguishable weave patterns were a form of group identification, or hallmark, then it is easy to understand that for as long as the preservation of a group's identity was desirable or possible, the distinguishing technique would remain. Variations of a minor order would exist and this is discussed under the subheading 'Variations or aberrations?' But major changes such as those that involved a change in motor habits would be unlikely to occur. Anyone who has seen a weaver at work is astonished at the speed with which the knots are tied. Such speed can only be achieved by an habitual mechanical process learnt in childhood and repeated so often that little thought is involved. Any change in the process would, of necessity, involve a clumsy transition. Nothing less than a fundamental change on such a scale as to break up these closely knit communities would result in the loss of a group's weaving technique.

A change of this sort came about, towards the end of the nineteenth century, with the advent of commercialism on a large and demanding scale and this did, in fact, disrupt and alter the traditional ways in many weaving centres. In these areas, what was traditional has now become commercial to the extent that group identity has been largely supplanted by national identity. 'Sennehs' are now made in Tehran, and so few modern 'Bakhtiaris' are made by the Bakhtiari people that some authors deny that they ever made rugs at all. In each case one can identify the genuine article, but increasingly is the label 'Made in Iran' superseding any valid description of ethnic or regional origin.

Weaving was a traditional occupation, and each group's individual method was passed on from mother to daughter as they worked side by side at the loom. Some explanations for the individual differences of technique are discussed below, although it seems impossible to say decisively how they arose. There is ample evidence, however, to show that the weavers of any group adhered more rigorously to their particular local technique of structure than to any other feature of manufacture, and the weave pattern became in a sense the group's handwriting or hallmark.

The weavers were very conscious of their techniques and, in many cases, introduced features whereby their work could be readily recognized. In some kinds of rugs, for example, the weft is almost invariably of a particular colour, such as the red or pink of the Qashqa'i, the blue of the Kashan, or the alternating white and pale blue of the Veramin. The Qashqa'i use a barberpole-coloured selvedge; the Baluchi use heavy cords as a side finish, the number varying from two to six but most commonly four; Chinese rugs, on the other hand, are notable for the absence of a selvedge.

Why would these people go to the trouble of dyeing the weft threads if it were not as a means of distinguishing their work from that of other groups? The dyeing of a weft achieved no structural advantage and practically it meant extra work. One can therefore safely conclude that it was a group's method of signing its work.

Mention was made earlier of the difference between the attitudes to their work of nomad or village weavers on the one hand, and urban manufactory weavers on the other hand. The woman in her tent or village house, working alone,or assisted by her daughters or other female members of the family,produced firstly the rugs and bags required for the family's daily needs and status. After that she wove goods to sell, and these were made in the same way as those she made for her own use. Her craft formed a part of her domestic role, and was strongly circumscribed by tradition. Weaving the designs in the manner of her people, she was in a sense signing the rugs with the identity of her people. It was not the individual whose identity counted, but that of the group.

Compare this to the activity and attitudes of the master-weaver in a manufactory. He may or may not have done much of the actual weaving himself, but he designed cartoons, chose colours and organized the weavers, men or women. Beyond the financial reward, this master-weaver worked for his own credit as an artist, and for the credit of his studio; the tribe or family did not come into it. When his signature was woven into a rug, personal identity superseded group identity, and folkcraft gave way to conscious visual art form. The cult of the artist has at this point begun. The products of most manufactories were not signed, and for this reason obviously no individual could achieve fame, but the manufactory could, and many set themselves very high standards which of course increased the commercial value of their products.

Although the attitudes of the weavers working in these separate circumstances were quite different, there are characteristics common to both. Group or personal identification was frequently established by means other than design, for example, by weaving a mark or signature into the rug or by using a weft or selvedge of a particular colour. The former methods are exemplified by the marks of the Hereke manufactory and the signature of master-weavers such as Serafian. The latter method is exemplified by the rugs of Amogli, the master-weaver of Meshed, who always made the selvedge in a particular blue colour. But beyond these conscious and deliberate means of identification is the weavers' handwriting, that is, the weave pattern.

Following the path indicated by the early experts such as Mumford and Hawley, dealers and students of Oriental rugs have acquired their knowledge of weave pattern from their own experience and by observing that a given design or certain number of designs is commonly associated with a particular weave pattern. It has been found, for example, that rugs with Tekke designs can be classified into one of two main weave pattern groups, from which it can be deduced that there are at least two identifiable Tekke weaves. Plate 75 shows one of these.

The name Kashan conjures up a picture of a very well-known type of Persian design. For those who have studied the backs of rugs, the name will also evoke a picture of a particular weave pattern, as shown in Plate 31.

These weave patterns are the only feature that can be used for the identification of rugs like the one illustrated in Plate 28. Portrait rugs, as they are called, and picture rugs are known to have been made in a number of towns, such as Isfahan, Kashan, Kerman and Tabriz, but where they were made can neither be established by the design alone nor solely by any other feature to be seen on the front of the rug. But they can be identified solely by reference to their reverse side because the weave pattern of a rug made in any one of those towns is distinctive from one made in any of the other towns. Similarly, the rug illustrated in Plate 8 has a design which is not traditional to any known rug-knotting centre and the rug may be unique. Therefore, whereas the design is of no assistance in determining the rug's provenance, the weave pattern is. The weave pattern of Plate 7 indicates that the rug is a Bijar and Plate 27 illustrates an Isfahan. The weave pattern of the Isfahans can be traced back as far as the so-called 'Indo-Isfahans' some of which were clearly made by Isfahan weavers. Here again we have a weave pattern that has remained recognizably constant for centuries.

In other centres social and economic upheavals have disrupted or completely broken the traditional sequence. An example is to be found in Ushak. The sixteenth and seventeenth-century rugs of this town have a distinctive weave pattern which no longer exists. The weave pattern of modern Ushaks is very different from that of the earlier ones. There are other rugs of the sixteenth and seventeenth centuries which have a distinctive weave pattern but because of a break in continuity and insufficient historical data, they cannot be attributed to a particular place of manufacture. Coupled with this problem is the knowledge that some towns made rugs during the classical era but later ceased manufacture. The town of Yezd in southern Iran once produced rugs which were widely acclaimed, but no surviving rug has yet been positively identified as a Yezd of the classical period, although we anticipate that research will one day link some of the seventeenth-century rugs of unknown provenance with Yezd.

Quality of the weave
So far, knotting technique has been discussed solely in the context of rug identification, but it is also relevant to quality. A common fallacy is to regard knot density as the predominant factor when determining value. A dealer, expert, and friend of the authors once remarked that some people would not buy a rug unless he could guarantee that the weaver went blind making it! In

fact, knot density is a matter of secondary importance. An examination of the quality of manufacture should be directed to the compactness and uniformity of the weave. One hears the words 'tight knotting' but this is not as good a term as 'compactness of weave'. Compactness means that the row, or rows of weft shoots have been firmly beaten or pressed down on the preceding row of knots, for it is the weft which keeps each row of knots in place. Any looseness of weft must inevitably result in the knots working loose, whether or not they are tied tightly to the warp.

Knot density is in fact a relative matter, and depends on a number of factors, one of which may be the technique used in construction; but different techniques do not necessarily mean different qualities. A Kazak with 100 knots per square inch would be one with a relatively high knot-density, whereas 150 knots to the square inch for a Nain would be very low, as the norm for the Nain is in excess of 500 (1 square inch = 0,0645 square decimetres). To illustrate this point, refer to the Kazak (Plate 33) and the Nain (Plate 51). The former has two or three thick weft threads between each row of knots, whereas the Nain has two very thin weft threads between each row. The diameter or size of the Kazak knots is three or four times that of the Nain because the yarn used in the Kazak is so much thicker. Despite the difference in the knot count, both examples are technically excellent, in that both are strongly made, compact fabrics.

It would be impossible to produce the Nain's finely drawn picture with the Kazak technique and the Kazak would look totally different if made in the Nain manner. Fine design detail can only be executed with small knots.

Local differences in weave pattern

An interesting and problematical question is why one technique became established in a particular area to the exclusion of all others. A large number of factors must have contributed to the development of local differences in weaving techniques, but only a few are accessible to study today. Most of these differences were probably historically determined, while others were influenced by the local availability of materials. For the most part we cannot make dogmatic statements about the reasons for one weave pattern being adopted or evolved in any particular area, but it is worthwhile looking at the factors which might have exercised an influence on the weaving technique of various areas.

Examination of the rugs of the Caucasus will show that as a general rule the higher the altitude at which the weavers lived and worked, the higher the pile of the rugs. The lower the altitude of the area, and therefore where protection from cold was not the primary consideration, the lower the pile. The manufacture of a high or low pile does not require a different basic technique because all that is involved is the clipping of the pile threads to the desired height. A high pile does, however, preclude a fine, precise design.

In the aöuls, or mountain villages, of the Caucasus where temperatures of forty degrees below freezing are not uncommon, warmth was the prime requisite and hence the thick yarn – which meant large knots – the long pile, and designs compatible with these features. Along the shores of the Caspian Sea, protection from cold was not a significant consideration, and therefore the rugs are low piled, enabling the weaver to execute more precise and detailed designs such as those of the Shirvans and Kubas. Compare the designs and weave of the Kazak (Plates 33, 34), the Chi Chi (Plates 11, 12) and the Seyshour (Plates 71, 72). The altitudes of derivation are respectively, high, middle and low.

Another factor which can determine the nature of the weave is the function for which the woven object is intended. The Anatolian Yürüks, who were nomads, made long-piled, flexible beds known as 'yataks', which were square and with a coarse weave. The Qashqa'i made among other things, very flexible knotted rugs as blankets. To achieve this, several additional weft shoots, sometimes as many as seven, were introduced between the rows of knots, and the result was a far more pliable fabric than if it had only one or two wefts.

The relationships between long pile and high altitude, and long pile and function cannot be regarded as generally applicable to rug weaving because it is in fact easier and quicker to make a long-piled rug with coarse knots, and therefore it will be found that bazaar rugs are all of that type. No short-clipped bazaar rugs will be found, as indifferent work is masked by long pile.

It is easier to see the operation of environmental factors on weaving techniques in groups which have moved from their original homes to a new area. Sections of a tribe or group would occasionally move voluntarily or were forced to move, and this separated them from the greater part of their own people. A splinter group, settled in a new area, would probably tend to be less tradition-bound, and therefore more receptive to a strong personality or other influences, all of which would tend to accelerate changes from the traditional. If, in addition, available dyes and materials were different from those they had previously been accustomed to then a change would be more marked. Such a group might on the other hand influence their new neighbours. In either of these circumstances a modified or new weave pattern could result.

An important movement of this kind occurred during the reign of the Ottoman dynasty which was firmly established in Turkey with its conquest of Byzantine Constantinople in 1453. The expansionist policy that followed included the occupation of Tabriz in 1514, 1534 and again later in the century. The first and second occupations brought the influence of Persian rug designs to Turkey with the importation of many of the famous weavers and other artisans of Tabriz. In the period that followed, Turkish workshops began to make floral and medallion carpets, and to use the Persian knot which is better suited to the execution of minute design detail and therefore to curvilinear patterns. The influence of Tabriz, where the art of the book developed and flourished, was very strong at this time, but the Turkish manufactories modified the Persian designs and colours, and this resulted in a recognizably Ottoman product, the weave patterns of which are distinguishable from the Tabriz fabrics of the same era.

A similar example of Persian influence on the carpet industry of Turkey was the use of the renowned weavers of Kerman in starting the Turkish Imperial Manufactory at Hereke in 1884. Here again, a distinctive product developed which can in no way be confused, on the basis of structure or weave pattern, with the equally famous products of Kerman itself.

How can this be explained? It was suggested earlier in this work that the master-weavers who organized the manufactories did very little of the actual weaving themselves. When a manufactory was established, and master-weavers were brought in from another area to organize it, their function was the training of local people and the teaching of designs. Very often, the outsiders introduced their colour and design sense, and both at Agra in India, during the sixteenth century, and at Hereke, during the nineteenth century, the manufactories started by weaving entirely Persian designs. In time the influence of the local feeling for colour and design grew stronger, and at Agra and the other Indian centres a distinctly Indian style developed, known usually by the name of the reigning dynasty, the Mughals. Hereke developed a use of colour which is typically Turkish, and considerably different from the Persian. The Hereke designs, however, continued to be derived from the Persian. What is significant is that in both these centres it was the local weavers, and not the foreigners, who evolved the precise method of weaving that was used by each manufactory and, as a result, the weave patterns of their products are identifiable, and are different from those of the towns or manufactories from where the original master-weavers came.

The position in India is somewhat different. The weave pattern of the so-called 'Indo-Isfahans' clearly shows that not only a master-weaver was imported from Isfahan, but also the weavers themselves. Another exception is to be found in Tabriz when Kerman weavers were brought in at the end of the last century to assist in the revival of the industry. For a period the rugs of Tabriz had a weave pattern that was almost indistinguishable from the rugs of Kerman.

Effect of political or environmental change

Even though tribal or local weaving techniques were not readily susceptible of change, changes did inevitably occur. A number of factors could be responsible, such as the influence of a foreign element adopted into a group by marriage, or a necessary adaptation to new materials as a result of migration. On the slender evidence available, it would seem likely that intermarriage did occur, though rarely, between members of different tribes, and possibly only as a result of conquest. Perhaps this could explain the existence of at least a few of the Turkoman 'hybrids' as, presumably, if a woman of a defeated Salor group,

36

for example, married a Tekke man, she would continue to use the technique she had learnt as a child from her own mother, but would now adopt the designs of her husband's people. We, of course, do not know if a situation of that sort ever in fact occurred, but it is described to illustrate a fundamental concept of this monograph, namely, that the rugs produced by a Salor woman forced into such a predicament would be correctly described as Salor, not Tekke. A Kerman design used in the Hereke manufactory would result, not in a Kerman rug, but a Hereke. In the art world we have the example of the processes of the law being used to prove that the Van Meegeren fakes of Vermeer's work were not Vermeers, but Van Meegerens. The attribution belongs to the maker, not to the source of the design, unless one seeks complete accuracy, in which event the rugs in our hypothetical case should be described as Salors with a Tekke design.

A radical change of a permanent nature, which took place as a result of adaptation to new materials, was that of the Ersari Turkoman tribe which migrated into present-day Afghanistan from the steppe lands east of the river, Amu Darya. Earlier this tribe seems to have been chased out of the Manguishlak Peninsula by the Yomut, and it then settled along the Amu Darya. The movement took place over a long period of time. Ersari tribes were encountered in what is now Afghanistan in the seventeenth century, but the southward migration continued until recently, and was given a final impetus by the Bolshevik Revolution. The Kharchin sheep, with their fine wool, which had formed the herds of the Ersari on the steppes, did not thrive in the mountainous country into which they moved, and were replaced by sheep providing a wool of a coarser fibre. As a result, the well-known Afghan Ersari carpets with their large, bold patterns and coarse weave, are noticeably different in appearance from the Ersari rugs of the steppes, that is, the rugs of the Ersari tribes who remained further north on the Amu Darya in what is now Soviet Turkmenistan. An environmental change of this nature could also affect the colour of materials used. A striking example of this is the type of rug known as Pendeh. These rugs have a background colour, variously described as liver or purplish-brown, which was derived from materials apparently only available in the area of the Pendeh oasis. Sections of most of the major Turkoman tribes at one time or another occupied land in this area and, while there, some of them used this particular dye. The name 'Pendeh' attached to a rug, therefore, says where it was made, but does not identify the tribe who wove it.

An interesting study, but one which can only be touched on here, is the effect of conquest on the weaving craft of the conquered people. As far as can be ascertained, weaving on a village or tribal level, generally continued despite political change. Azadi (1975) says: 'The manufacturing techniques (choice of wool, spinning, twisting, blending and dyeing) and the structure (warp, weft, pile and other features) were unaffected by victory or defeat or at any rate there is no evidence that the victors attempted to enforce adherence to their own techniques' (p. 33). Court manufactories and other urban workshops were understandably more readily affected by political change, and that of Isfahan, which had been established by Shah Abbas the Great in the last decade of the sixteenth century, closed completely after the Afghan invasion in 1722 which brought to an end the reign of the Safavid dynasty. Unlike the traditional folkcraft, the state manufactories were very dependent on the character and taste of the reigning monarch of the time. Erdmann (1962) points out that, with the few exceptions of Herat and certain workshops in Kerman and north-western Persia, the eighteenth century witnessed the collapse of carpet production in Persia, and this was probably due, according to Erdmann, to the fact that the 'sixteenth century "golden age" had concentrated all of its energies in the city manufactories. By this means these were rendered capable of magnificent feats, but at the same time the smaller shops and peasant production, which might have been able to preserve the tradition and carry on when the great workshops collapsed, were sorely hurt' (p. 45).

A strange and interesting, though sad, case of what could happen as a result of conquest was that of the Salor Turkomans. In the late eighteenth and early nineteenth centuries, the various groups of Salor, those near the Persian border and those who were living further east, near Pendeh, suffered defeat at the hands of the Persians, the Saryk and the Tekke, and where they had once been the most powerful Turkoman tribe, they were now scattered and reduced to political insignificance. Some of them were absorbed by the conquering tribes.

The curious thing is that although the smaller, flatter Salor gul lived on in the weavings of the Saryk and Tekke, it appears as if the distinctive Salor weave disappeared altogether. Compared to other changes that have taken place in Turkoman weaving, the disappearance of the Salor weave, and with it, the distinctive, subtle use of colour, was quite sudden. In his 1908 publication, Bogolyubov (1973) writes: 'I have heard it said that the Salors do not weave carpets any more because the Persian Khans, when they became their new masters, confiscated all their better products and more or less forced them to give up their traditional occupation' (p. 19). Certainly the famous Salor gul continued to be used largely by the Tekke and Saryk tribes, and is still used today, but the weave patterns and colour of these rugs are those of the tribes who wove them, not of the Salor. This apparent cessation of weaving was probably not at all typical of conquered people, and this must then be seen as an extreme case, and possibly unique.

We feel that it is necessary to point out at this stage that the Salor weave pattern which disappeared so suddenly is that which is exemplified by the fragment in the Museum of Fine Arts, Boston, (Plates 61, 62) and the Salor juval which is Item 1a in the carpet study section of the Textile Department of the Victoria and Albert Museum, London. Another group of rugs with the Salor gul of smaller and flatter shape and with a weave pattern distinct from that of any other Turkoman group, may constitute another Salor weave pattern that lived on somewhat longer. But this remains an hypothesis for further study.

On the evidence available, conquerors seem to have had less influence on the weaving craft than had market forces. Although the Russian presence in southern Caucasia in the early nineteenth century was that of conqueror, it was rather in their milder role of wealthy buyers that the Russians influenced Caucasian rug designs. Traditional designs continued to be woven in the Caucasus, but European fashion intruded in the form of commissions for carpets bearing Aubusson designs, or modifications of these, because the foreign purchasers felt them to be better suited to the French furniture which was fashionable at the time. This seems to have affected the rugs of the Karabagh region more than any other part of the Caucasus. European influence was very strongly felt also in

Persia, in areas such as Kerman, Bijar (Plate 8) and Senneh. However, in none of these places where alien designs were introduced in the nineteenth century were the techniques of manufacture affected and the Karabaghs, Bijars and others, made in these completely uncharacteristic designs, are nonetheless identifiable by virtue of their structural features, particularly the weave pattern.

Nomenclature

An adherence to weave pattern is the most stable feature in an art form that has pervaded a large area of the world since at least the third century B.C. The most mutable feature is the nomenclature that has been used to describe the examples of the craft. The reason is partly found in man's ingenuity, partly in his ignorance, and partly in his need for accuracy – as strange as that may seem in view of the confusion that has resulted.

Many more names have been added to the list since the time of the early writers such as Martin and Mumford. Some of these names are descriptive of design, some denote provenance, and some are used solely to differentiate between qualities of the same type. A few names have lost favour because a consensus of opinion regarded them as inaccurate; a few of the same group are still used because habits are hard to break. The use of 'Kabistan' is still fairly common among the doyens of the rug trade. Although they are aware of the incorrect derivation of the name, they are equally aware that the modern classification of Caucasian rugs is far from satisfactory. The word 'Kabistan' is meaningful to them, and they will continue to' use it, despite the denial in many texts of their scholarly right to do so. Another name that refuses to die, but which has even less right to existence, is 'Royal Bokhara'. Where the name came from, nobody knows, but custom, Hawley, mystique, and snob appeal have prolonged its life unnecessarily. Hawley (1970) refers to three types of rug – Royal Bokhara, Princess Bokhara and Tekke Bokhara (p. 239). Today, we know that all three were made by the Tekke tribe, and they were neither royal, nor necessarily from the Khanate of Bokhara.

A need for accuracy has created names for subdivisons of a group, but whether or not the objective is achieved depends solely on the user. In this regard, the example of the Hamadan weaving area provides the most striking illustration. There must be many hundreds of villages in the Hamadan area, and many of these adhere to their own traditional design. Structurally, these rugs are the same, but the area is so large that purchaser and seller alike would be far from satisfed if the whole group were bundled together under a single name, 'Hamadan'. The rugs would also be far more difficult to sell! As a result, village names are given to particular designs, and one should therefore call these names subdivisions of the Hamadan class.

The same sort of problem arises in the Caucasus. Here it is aggravated by arbitrary geographical divisions that are used, but cannot be precisely or even remotely defined, although attempts are made to do so. A glance at the map will illustrate the point. In the eastern part of the Caucasus we find the Daghestan district in the north, the town of Kuba roughly in the middle, and the district of Shirvan to the south. There are Daghestan rugs, Kuba rugs and Shirvan rugs, but to assume, or assert, that there is any clear geographical demarcation between the areas where they are made, is quite untenable. On the basis of weave pattern, certain broad areas of manufacture can be demonstrated, but the weave pattern cannot differentiate between a Chi Chi, a Kuba or a Shirvan, for example. Hawley (1970) said that '. . . nearly every class has a typical weave differentiating it from all other classes' (p. 50).

But Hawley did not define a class and nor do we intend to do so. The point is that a name seldom denotes a class, no matter what meaning one places on the word. And no one has, and nor will anyone seriously maintain that one can differentiate between each named type by its weave. All that Hawley meant was that weave differences provide a valid basis for classification.

The problem of nomenclature is further complicated by using the same name to describe two rugs of very different weave pattern. This is done sometimes in ignorance or because a name has come to describe a quality, and sometimes for reprehensible reasons. 'Sarouk' is an example of a name which is used to mean two very distinct rugs. It is used to describe the best quality rug from the Sultanabad weaving complex which was created by commercial enterprise at the end of the last century. These rugs do not remotely resemble the great rugs, formerly made in the village of that name north-west of Sultanabad, which have a prior claim to the use of the name 'Sarouk'.

The label 'Salor' is all too frequently used for rugs that display the Salor gul but not a Salor weave pattern. This is done either in ignorance or deliberately in order to place a higher value on the piece concerned. The fact that the Salor gul has been copied by other tribes should be widely and generally known by dealers, and yet these 'Salors' are frequently sold as the genuine article when the weave pattern clearly indicates some other origin, usually Saryk. This sort of problem is unwittingly aided and abetted by careless statements from those who should know better. A recent publication of otherwise immense value includes the statement: 'To recognise the gul is to know the tribe that produced the rug.' There is more than adequate evidence to prove this statement completely wrong.

Names are used loosely, sometimes with the facility of detachable labels, and the reason lies not solely in the ignorance of the user but also in that there is no established or universally accepted record of their meaning. Apart from that, there is the fact that nomenclature is a changeable concept, and therefore names frequently mean different things to different people.

Weave pattern: the most stable feature
A classification by weave pattern will not resolve all of these complexities, but, except where a rug has been repiled, the weave pattern remains an immutable feature and will provide a stable feature of reference, unlike selvedges that are replaced and ends that wear away. We have demonstrated that a weave pattern is the manifest and permanent record of a rug's origin. It may have originated in a large area comprising many villages making rugs of differing designs, or in a single village which produces a number of designs. In the former instance, the weave pattern will not indicate the village of origin, but the design may, if it is the exclusive property of that village and has not been copied elsewhere. A lack of historical records or an incomplete analysis of existing knowledge can and does, in rare instances, result in the isolation of a distinctive weave pattern which cannot be attributed to a particular place or people. For example, a

Zel-i-Sultan design and weave pattern can be recognized as a product separate and distinct from any other group. Precisely where, and by whom Zel-i-Sultan rugs were made nevertheless remains a matter for conjecture. The evidence points to the area between Sarouk and the Feraghan valley, but no more positive attribution is possible at present. Although this example is not unique, similar examples are rare, but without the aid of the weave pattern, rugs of this type would be incorrectly allocated to one or other group of known weavers, an error which, as we have suggested elsewhere, has occurred in the classification of some Turkoman rugs.

The importance of the weave pattern lies not in the desire to reclassify rugs according to structure, but in the fact that this feature remains the single most valuable aid in determining who the weavers were, or where they came from. A positive identification of provenance has been, and remains, the central theme in discussions on rugs, a theme that engages academics, dealers and collectors alike. The methodology of studying Oriental rugs must therefore include an examination of weave pattern and to a greater degree than has been the case in the past. Some authorities on the rugs of the classical era have not omitted this feature. For example, Erdmann (1970), discussing a seventeenth-century rug found in India, says: 'Because of its *structure* [our italics], colouring and design, especially that of its border, this must be assigned to the group of Persian Vase carpets probably from Kerman in South Persia' (p.70).

Many other authorities, academic and dealer alike, manifest a tendency to prefer design features when faced with problems of provenance. This tendency is always suspect, but becomes even more so when one realizes that the decline in artistic expression in the craft after the seventeenth century, and which accelerated during this century, was accompanied by an ever-increasing proclivity to copy designs that were commercially successful. The tendency still remains, and sometimes attempts to support it are made by arguing that if the weave pattern does not accord with the chosen provenance, then the weave pattern must be an aberration.

Variations or aberrations?

The products we are dealing with are made by the hands of man, not by machines, and therefore deviations from the normal type are to be expected. But the word 'aberration' is too readily used instead of establishing through proper research the reason for eccentricity.

Deviations from the norm can, and do, patently occur as the result of varying degrees of skill in the application of the technique required. It is not uncommon to find skilful and unskilful work in the same rug. This may occur as the result of teacher and pupil working on the same piece, or merely because of varying degrees of application exerted at different times. The more one examines weave patterns, the more one becomes aware of this type of variation, but they are all nevertheless, readily recognizable as the weave pattern of a particular group. What the sceptics must realize is that these variations, or aberrations, are not of such a degree that one will find a Hamadan with a Kashan weave, or a Kuba with a Kazak weave, or a Salor with an Ersari weave – to name a few impossibilities. Designs were widely borrowed but never the totality of the technique of manufacture.

The variations to be seen in the same rug may be deliberate, for example, border areas woven in a technique different from the main area. This is not an uncommon method of giving greater strength to an area normally subjected to the most wear. The border technique may not be typical of the group's weave pattern, but the combination of the two may well be typical, for example, the short extra wefts to be found on the sides of Talish rugs.

An interesting example of two techniques in one rug, both of which are representative of the same area, is a Melayer photographed for the authors' records. The major portion of this rug is made in the single-wefted technique typical of the northern part of Melayer, with interpolated bands of various widths in a double-wefted technique typical of the style found in southern Melayer. The explanation for this combination is not known. It could be the work of a helpful visitor who is accustomed to working in the other technique, a display of versatility on the part of one weaver, or an unconscious reference to a previous habit.

Whether or not a weave pattern is an aberration of a known group of weavers or is representative of some other group, possibly unidentified, can only be established by reference to sufficient examples to substantiate a conclusion. The further back in time one goes the less possible does this become because of insufficient surviving examples. In theory that gloomy statement appears to be indisputable until one examines the facts. It is true that pictures are all that remain of some rugs of the past, but a lot of rugs that have been referred to and illustrated in early publications are well preserved in museums or private collections. Some examples from previous eras have survived because they were representative of a type or, more important, because they were treasured possessions – treasured because of the quality of both their conception and execution. With regard to their execution, two or three rugs with the same weave pattern would indicate to us, if not to the cynics, that the weave pattern is not an aberration. In this context fragments of rugs can be of great assistance for purposes of comparison.

From the eighteenth century onwards more examples survive and obviously many more inferior articles survive. The quantity may make the task of comparison more onerous but at the same time if properly undertaken it will make the conclusions relatively more valid.

Where nothing but illustrations survive one is forced to refer to the only evidence available, but at the same time one must be conscious that the evidence is suspect as it is not the best evidence. How frequently is one referred both in text and conversation to an illustration of a rug in support of a disputed identification. This usually occurs with regard to a unique or at least very uncommon design. But how much more valid would the reference be if one were able to compare both design and weave pattern. Under the entry 'Turkoman' in the dictionary, we have mentioned a too-eager tendency to classify according to known categories when the weave pattern indicates either an aberration or an attribution that has not yet been identified. We have no doubt that an obligation to show the front and the weave pattern of every rug illustrated would be rewarded by something far more positive and interesting than the label 'provenance unknown'.

Methodology of identification

So far we have confined our argument to one aspect of weave, namely, the visible conformation of structure which forms a pattern. We have deliberately omitted a technical analysis of the materials because, whilst we fully acknowledge that a technical analysis is a *sine qua non* of a proper description of a textile, on its own it is very little more than descriptive and has limited value in determining the origin of an Oriental rug. We will explain this assertion but before doing so we will briefly outline the way in which a rug is structured.

Every woven fabric is the result of interweaving two sets of threads. Various names are used for these threads but for our purposes we will confine ourselves to the terms 'warp' and 'weft'. The warp threads are those that extend lengthways and are the first threads to be used in the process. They are fixed to the loom and whatever number is used remains constant throughout manufacture. The warp threads are under tension throughout the weaving process and therefore they must have sufficient tensile strength to take this strain. The strength is imparted by a high degree of twist, this being an essential element of a thread because without twist it would have no strength. An increase in twist increases strength up to the point where further twist would rupture the fibres and thus weaken the thread.

At one time the direction of a yarn's twist was referred to as 'left' or 'right' which is a poor description as the direction indicated depends entirely on the aspect of the observer. The universal description used nowadays is 'Z' or 'S' spun. The wefts are woven transversely into the warps in regular or irregular succession passing over and under alternate warps. The aggregate number of wefts increases as the work progresses. A kelim is made solely of warp and weft. A knotted rug on the other hand includes knots which are tied laterally in rows as the weaving advances. The two ends of the knot threads form the pile.

There are three basic knots: the Spanish knot which is wrapped round one warp thread; the symmetrical knot, also referred to as the closed, Turkish or Ghiordes knot; and the asymmetrical knot, also referred to as the open, Persian or Senneh knot. Unlike the Spanish knot each symmetrical or asymmetrical knot is tied to two warp threads. What we would like to call an aberration but is

46

too commonplace for that description is the deceitful jufti knot which is tied to four warps. The use of the jufti is universally deplored except by the users who find they can cover the same area with half the effort. The economy in effort is achieved at the expense of a great loss in quality.

A number of rugs begin and end with a web of kelim. If no kelim is used then the rug begins with the insertion of weft threads after which the rows of knots begin. Usually a weft is introduced after every one or two rows of knots. Sometimes a single weft thread is used as in the Hamadan group; in other rugs the number may be two or three or more and whatever number is used may be in a regular or irregular succession. The weft is then beaten down on the preceding row of knots, the degree to which this is done determining the compactness of the end-product. The number of wefts used between the rows of knots is a factor contributing to the flexibility of the woven article. We have mentioned that the Qashqa'i make a knotted fabric as a blanket and in order to obtain a degree of flexibility greater than would be required in a carpet, more wefts are used – as many as seven have been found.

After a number of rows of knots have been completed, the knot ends are cut to the desired height of the pile. A carpet with a finely worked design will have a very low pile to reveal the design to best advantage. Where warmth or a comfortable surface is required the pile will be longer.

On the back of the carpet one can see the nodes of the knots, each knot having a pair. Where the knots are tied in such a way that the warp threads lie on the same plane the two nodes are visible side by side. Where the knots are tied so that one of the two warps to which a knot is tied lies directly under the other, one sees only one of the two nodes. Examples of this type of depressed warp are the Bijar (Plate 7) and the Kerman (Plate 35), and in both these types of rug a depressed warp is the norm. In between the even-plane warps and those like the Bijar are intermediate degrees of depression as in the Kula (Plate 45) and the Daghestan (Plate 13). In both of these types a degree of depression is the norm.

Technical analysts of rugs describe the materials used, how they are spun, how the spun yarns are plied, the type of knot used and whether or not a warp is depressed. These descriptions vary in the extent of the information provided and are generally composed of a combination of symbols and literal descriptions. As yet no one appears to have devised a system of recording all the relevant facts disclosed by an analysis of the weave. An example of a technical analysis is:

Warp – Z2S wool in ivory, dark natural mixtures; two levels.
Weft – Z2S wool in natural mixtures; a band dyed red; two shots.
Pile – 2Z wool; Ghiordes-knotted, pile slanting to the left.

This description means that the warp is made of Z-spun wool two threads of which are plied in an S direction. The weft is the same composition and two weft threads pass after each row of knots. The knot used is the symmetrical (Ghiordes), and the yarn with which the knots are made comprises two Z-spun threads. The pile slants to the left. From this description of the pile and the stated fact that the warps are on two levels, one can deduce that the left-hand warp of the two warps to which a knot is tied is depressed so that the knot ends protrude from between the warps on the left side of the weaver.

A more sophisticated method is used by an authority who has devised a more detailed description of the knots recognizing that the nodes can lie either consistently at right angles to the warp lines or consistently at an acute angle – we draw attention to this feature in the plates. The knots are described as SY1, SY2 and SY3 for the symmetrical knots and AS1, AS2, AS3 and AS4 for the asymmetrical knots. For the purpose of our discussion the definition of these symbols is irrelevant and is therefore omitted. Using this method of description four examples will be discussed:

1 Warp – wool, S-plied, 2 strands, twisted, undyed ivory.
   Weft – wool, Z-plied, 1 to 2 strands, not twisted, undyed ivory to grey-brown, 2 shoots, both waved, alternating.
   Pile – wool, Z-plied, 2 strands, not twisted, knots AS2.
2 Warp – wool, S-plied, 2 strands, twisted, undyed light ivory.
   Weft – wool, Z-plied, 2 strands, not twisted, undyed light brown, 2 shoots, both waved.
   Pile – wool, Z-plied, 2 strands, not twisted, knots AS2.
3 Warp – wool, S-plied, 2 strands, twisted, undyed brown.

Weft – Z-plied, 2 strands, not twisted, undyed light ivory, 2 shoots, both waved.

Pile – wool, Z-plied, 2 strands, not twisted, knots AS2.

4 Warp – wool, S-plied, 2 strands, twisted, grey-brown.

Weft – wool, Z-plied, 2 strands, not twisted, undyed brown, 2 shoots, both waved.

Pile – wool, Z-plied, 2 strands, not twisted, knots AS2.

A consideration of these four examples will show that the warps of all of them are made of S-plied wool, two strands and twisted; the wefts of all of them are two strands of Z-plied, undyed, untwisted wool; the pile threads in each case are AS2 knotted with two threads of Z-plied untwisted wool. The colour descriptions of the yarns vary slightly but the degree is entirely a subjective test and therefore cannot be used as an empirical criterion of differentiation.

The four examples taken are an Ersari, a Tekke, a Chaudor and a Yomut respectively. It is apparent that the analysis of the structure of these rugs is inadequate to differentiate between the four types whereas a comparison of the weave patterns illustrated in Plates 15, 75, 9 and 79 will clearly show how different they are.

We must stress that we are not criticizing the methods of structural analysis. Analyses are important, but on their own they cannot be used as a methodology to establish provenance, nor, we must add, does the authority who uses the method in the examples claim that they can. The reason lies in the fact, already pointed out, that all the relevant facts are not disclosed. What is also of relevance are the degree of twist; varying thicknesses in the same yarn resulting from the method of spinning; the conformation and angle of the knots; and whether or not the weft is visible. These features are some of the elements which in various combinations constitute differing and traditional ways of weaving, and compose a weave pattern which is visibly different from that of other weaving groups.

Therefore any methodology used for the identification of Oriental rugs should ideally include a structural analysis , a design analysis, a colour analysis, an analysis of side and end finishes, and it must include an illustration of the weave pattern. All that Mumford and Hawley were saying was that the only one of those features which can be used in isolation is the weave pattern. We have already pointed out that the weave pattern will not identify a design subdivision of a group but it will show if the article is a Feraghan or a Sarouk, for example.

The craft in the twentieth century
In any picture of the changes that have occurred in the folkcraft during this century two predominant features must stand out. The one is the increase in commercialism and the other the waning of traditional culture.

From the turn of the century we have seen the rise of weaving centres that were conceived solely by commercial enterprise. These centres were in themselves a breach with tradition because their only motivation was production for an alien market, a far cry from the manufactories that were primarily concerned with court patronage and only incidentally with foreign commissions. For example, Sultanabad was almost solely concerned with the Western market; the manufactories of Pakistan date from 1947 and were set up to earn much-needed foreign exchange; the first manufactory was set up in Afghanistan in the 1960s; Smyrna, the Sultanabad of Turkey, is predominantly concerned with production for export to the West. These centres were all orientated to the requirements of the West which meant not only adapting designs to suit the market but producing designs in colours that were more acceptable to the alien purchasers.

Some forty years ago the Iran Carpet Company was incorporated as a government-sponsored body 'to rationalize the industry', in the words of the Company's president. Here again the interference by the government was a radical change from the situation of a rural peasant making a rug for sale when the need arose, or a manufactory that relied entirely on its own judgement of traditional taste as opposed to those turning out designs dictated to it by outsiders. This rationalization has served to transfer the craft from that of a regional folkcraft to the realms of a national industry. For example, state-sponsored manufactories wherever situated will make designs that were traditional to one or more other centres. It no longer follows that a name of a rug which bears the name of a tribe or place carries the built-in warranty that it was made by that tribe or in that place. Today the sole warranty is that it is handmade in Iran, or Turkey or Afghanistan. But what does one call a Bakhtiari design made in Isfahan? On the tenets of our argument we would be obliged to call it an Isfahan but we would be out of step with every commercial house dealing in these products.

We have been dealing with commercialism as it has affected traditional designs but it has also radically affected the traditional weave patterns and created new ones. Manufactories are concerned with production on the most economical basis and the implementation of that precept means conformity not only in the technique of production, but also in the commodity produced. If a manufactory complex is obliged to import weavers from other areas it would hardly be acceptable if they all used their own home-grown techniques. It may be that places such as Sultanabad have purposely developed their own technique as a distinguishing feature.

In Turkey another factor has arisen to break down the traditional ways. The government started weaving-schools to revive the craft and thereby to reduce poverty and earn foreign exchange. One of the results has been the ever-increasing prevalence of a uniform weave pattern throughout Turkey.

Disregarding the economic pressures that militate against a prolonged life for the craft one can foresee the probability of all commercially orientated weaving centres developing their own distinguishing techniques and maintaining them as a matter of pride. If this were to happen then at least as far as techniques are concerned there could be a re-creation of regional differences on a structural basis. Whether or not regional differences in designs will ever be restored is another matter.

Dictionary

ABADEH *Persian, Map: 17*
Manufactory rugs have been made in the village of Abadeh for approximately forty years. The designs of these robust rugs are largely influenced by those of the Qashqa'i and other tribes in the area.

ABDAL *Turkoman, Central Asia*
Even though no rugs have been positively identified as the products of this Turkoman clan, the name is included because the Abdal were known to have been weavers and recent research indicates that some pieces of doubtful identification, particularly in the Yomut group, may well be the work of these people. Plate 10 in Azadi's *Turkoman Carpets* illustrates a carpet which he assigns to the Arabatchi, Igdyr or Abdal. See Yomut.

ADRASKAND *Afghanistan*
The name does not appear to have been used by anyone other than Hartley Clark[1] and Dilley.[2] Hartley Clark maintained that these rugs came from the Adraskand valley south of Herat. He attributed them to a group which he called the 'South Western Afghanistan Group'. In this group he placed the Afghan Sabzawar (which is distinct from the Persian Sabzawar) and those rugs known by the rather loose term, 'Siyar-kar' meaning 'dark work'. He added that there were 'further sub-divisions merging into the Belouchistan proper'. Judging from his illustration a Belouch attribution would be favoured today for the entire group including the Adraskand. See Sabzawar and Siyar-kar.

AFGHAN *Turkoman and Afghan, Plates 15, 16*
The name is applied to two very different types of rugs, firstly, to the traditional products of Turkoman tribes, mainly Ersaris, who were migrating from as early as the seventeenth century into what became Afghanistan. Secondly, it applies to modern rugs made in Afghanistan manufactories with designs which are derived from the traditional ones of the Ersari, Beshir, Salor, Tekke, Yomut and Saryk. These are made not

only by Turkoman weavers, but also by Afghans who are not Turkoman and have no tradition of carpet knotting, but learnt it from the Turkoman tribes.

O'Bannon[3] divides the modern products of Afghanistan into three main categories: Mauri, Ersari carpets of Afghan and Khiva designs, and other Ersari patterns. He subdivides these groups on the basis of design as follows:

1 Mauri
    Herat, Maurchaq, Mazar-i-Sharif, Sariq, Zahir Shahi, Beshire, Torba Gul. (All of these names are used as prefixes to Mauri which is derived from the name Merv.)
2 Ersari of Afghan and Khiva designs
    Under this heading he gives one name, Daulatabad, with three subdivisions, Taghan, Suleiman and Dali.
3 Other Ersari
    Kunduz (Alti-Bolagh, Andkhoi and Shiberghan), Charshangu, Chob Bash, Beshire, Labijar, Kizil Ayak, Waziri, Karkin, and Naksha-i-Gashta.

The following list is taken from the catalogue published by the Afghan Carpet Export Guild, Kabul, Afghanistan, of an exhibition of modern Afghan handwoven carpets held in Kabul in May 1975.
'Provinces and Kinds of Carpets:
1 Herat
    Mauri (single and double thread), Sarooqi, Baluchi, Old Herati.
2 Badghis
    Mauri (single and double thread), Sarooqi, Akhal, Yamoodi, Salor.
3 Faryab
    Mauri (single and double thread), Baluchi, Daulatabadi, Altibulak.

4 Balkh
    Mauri (single and double thread), Dali, Taghan, Aranji, Sulimani.
5 Juzjan
    Lebjar, Saltoq, Qizilayaq, Chakish, Chubash, Chiqchi, Qazan, Farukh, Jangal Ariq, Charshang Gho, Dali, Uzbakya.
6 Samangan
    Kaldari.
7 Kunduz
    Qalai Zal, Qulukhtepe-i, Basheri.
8 Farah
    Baluchi.
9 Nimroz
    Baluchi.
10 Kabul
    New designs and some other kinds.'

It is to be noted that the spelling in the catalogue differs considerably from O'Bannon's spelling of the same names.

AFSHAN-CHILA *Caucasian*
Design classification of a Caucasian rug from the Baku area. See Baku.

AFSHAR *Persian, Map: J8*
These rugs have for a long time been made by the section of this tribe which lives a semi-nomadic life between Shiraz and Kerman. There are two other smaller Afshar groups, one near Bijar and the other near Lake Urmia where the main body of the tribe lived prior to their deportation by Shah Tahmasp in the sixteenth century. These two smaller groups do not seem to weave rugs, or if they do, their products do not appear to be distinguishable from those of the southern group.

The Afshar tribe was among those listed as

54

the clans of Turkoman Oghuz, in the eleventh century by Mahmud Kashghari and by Rashid al-din[4] in the thirteenth century. Nadir Shah, who was Shah of Iran from 1736 to 1747, was an Afshar.

Kouhi Afshar, 'kouhi' meaning 'from the mountains', is a term used to indicate an Afshar rug of superior quality.

The Afshar village rugs mentioned by Edwards[5] and other authors are: Balvardi (not to be confused with Bilverdi which is in the Heriz area) Kutlu, Dashtab, Deh Shotoran, Saarabad, Al-Saadi, Parizi, Dehaj, Beilleri and Morgi. See Saidabad.

Afshar rugs are distinctive both in design and weave.

AFYON *Anatolian*
Village in western Anatolia where rugs are woven. These are usually sold under the names of Karahisar or Isparta.

AGRA *Indian, Map: R9*
Type of rug from the Uttar Pradesh state in northern India. The city of Agra was the Mughal capital from 1566 to 1569 and again from 1601 to 1658, and is the site of the Taj Mahal built in the seventeenth century. Manufactory rugs have been made in Agra since the Mughal period, and it is probable that some of the great carpets of the Mughal period were made there. Many Agra carpets of the seventeenth and eighteenth centuries fall into the group known as 'Indo-Isfahan' which is discussed under the entry 'Mughal'. Some authorities use 'Indo-Isfahan' and 'Agra' as interchangeable terms but this is incorrect, as they ignore the fact that other Mughal cities produced carpets of the

Indo-Isfahan type. It is also incorrect because the name 'Agra' may also refer to carpets made since the eighteenth century; these carpets had developed an Indian style of design distinct from the earlier ones, though usually derived from them. These latter carpets also have a weave pattern that persists today, and which is very different from those of the Indo-Isfahan and Mughal periods.

AHAR *Persian, Map: G4*
Rug weaving town north of Heriz. The name is often prefixed to Heriz to denote a superior quality rug from this area. These rugs are structurally in the Heriz class.

AHMEDABAD *Persian*
Village in Iranian Azerbaijan which has given its name to a modern type of rug made in the area. These rugs are of the Karaje type.

AINABAD *Persian*
See Hamadan.

AINA-KAP *Turkoman*
Small bag used to hold a mirror.

AINALU *Persian*
See Khamseh Confederation.

AK-JOLI *Turkoman*
Decorative horse blanket.

AKHAL
See Afghan.

AKHAL TEKKE *Turkoman, Map: K5*
In the first half of the nineteenth century two main bodies of Tekke were known, one

living around the Akhal oasis and the other around the Merv oasis. Although two distinguishable Tekke weave patterns are known, and more may be identified, present knowledge cannot identify either with any particular geographic or ethnographic division of the tribe. See Tekke.

AKHISAR *Anatolian, Map: A3*
Although rugs from this village near Bergama have been known throughout this century, and may well have been made earlier, the production is small and few, if any, reach Western markets.

AKSTAFA *Caucasian, Map: G3, Plates 1, 2*
Town about ten kilometres north-east of the town of Kazakh. Although far closer to the Kazak weaving areas, Schürmann[6] includes these rugs in the Shirvan group. In structure they are certainly closer to Shirvan than to Kazak. The name is associated with a very distinctive design.

AKSU *East Turkestan, Map: R4*
According to Hubel[7] the name is, or was, used as a quality and design description for rugs sold in the town of this name in East Turkestan roughly 45°N and 70°E. He adds that the town was a collecting point for nomad rugs 'for many leagues around'. No other corroborative information can be found.

AKTY-MIKRA *Caucasian*
Derbend rugs at one time had a bad name and this induced the Russians to sell them under the name of Akty-Mikra. These rugs are now sold as 'Dagestanian', but they bear

no relationship to the true old Daghestans other than that they both come from the eastern Caucasus. See Derbend.

ALIABAD *Persian*
Village near Kashan, which produces rugs infrequently sold under this name, more frequently sold as Kashan.

ALLAHABAD *Indian, Map: S10*
Manufactory rugs produced in the city of that name situated at the junction of the Ganga and Yamuna Rivers. The city was founded in 1583 by the Emperor Akbar, and rugs were probably first made there about the same time.

ALPAN-KUBA *Caucasian*
See Kuba.

AL-SAADI *Persian*
See Afshar.

ALTI-BOLAGH (ALTIBULAK) *Afghan*
Name for a type of modern rug which O'Bannon classifies as Kunduz.[8] Eiland[9] says that these rugs are made in the Andkhoi area of Afghanistan. See Afghan.

ALVAND (ELVAND) *Persian, Map, see Mount Elwund: H6*
See Hamadan.

AMADABAD *Indian*
Seventeenth-century brocaded rug from the Indian town of that name situated in west-central India on the Sabermati River in the state of Gujarat. This name is not to be confused with the Ahmedabad which comes

from Azerbaijan, north-western Iran.

AMALEH *Persian*
See Qashqa'i.

AMOGLI (EMOGLI) *Persian*
Master-weaver who worked in Meshed and
died at the beginning of the twentieth
century. His rugs were made in the Khorasan
technique and frequently signed. They can be
distinguished from other Khorasans by their
blue selvedge which Amogli used for that
purpose. His son today still works in the
Meshed area.

AMRITSAR *Indian, Map: Q7*
Type of manufactory carpet from India of
which a sixteenth-century example is
illustrated by F.R. Martin.[10] See Bharistan.

AMSAGIRD *Persian*
See Hamadan.

ANATOLIAN
'Anatolia', meaning 'the land of the rising
sun', was the name of the Asian portion of
the country now called Turkey. The
description 'Anatolian' is one of those names
of last resort used when no more specific
identification is known, other than that the
rug was made in Turkey.

ANDKHOI *Afghan*
One of the modern Afghan rugs which
O'Bannon classifies under the name
'Kunduz'.

ANTALYA *Anatolian*
Rugs from the area around Antalya near

Doçemealti in Turkey.

ARAB
See Belouch and Khamseh Confederation.

ARABATCHI *Turkoman, Central Asia*
Tribe of the Arabatchi lived on the lower
reaches of the river Amu Darya. The remarks
made under the entry 'Abdal' apply equally
to the Arabatchi. See Yomut.

ARAB BELOUCH
See Belouch.

ARAK *Persian, Map, see Sultanabad: H6*
This city used to be called Sultanabad. As
applied to rugs the name denotes a medium
grade of rug from the Sultanabad area.

ARANJI
See Afghan.

ARDEBIL *Persian, Map: H4/H5*
Modern manufactory rugs in a design called
'Caucasian derivative' are made in the area
surrounding the town of this name.

ARDEBIL CARPET *Persian*
This carpet, housed in the Victoria and Albert
Museum in London, bears the Arabic date
A.H. 946 which, according to the Gregorian
calendar, is A.D. 1540. It is now believed to
have been made in Tabriz, but it is extremely
doubtful that it was made for the Ardebil
Mosque as originally supposed. The
sixteenth-century mosque in Ardebil did not
at that time have a room of sufficient
dimensions to accommodate the carpet which
measures 10,6 m by 5,4 m (34 ft 6 in. by 17 ft

6 in.) The mystery is deepened by the existence of a second carpet, a twin to the Ardebil, which was discovered in 1914 and subsequently purchased by the late John Paul Getty. It is believed that this second carpet had been cannibalized to repair the Ardebil sometime before the Museum bought it in 1893.

ARMENIAN *Map: G4*
Theoretically, this is either a rug made by an Armenian or a rug that comes from Armenia; practically, it is a rug from the Caucasus believed to have been made by an Armenian. Armenia borders on the Kazak weaving area of the Caucasus, and it is very likely that a number of the so-called 'Kazak' rugs were made by Armenians. The fact that several of these contain cruciform symbols and Christian dating, supports this belief. It is, however, not possible to isolate an Armenian category, either on the basis of design or structure, though there can be no doubt that Armenians did weave rugs. In early literature the dragon rugs of the Caucasus were referred to as 'Armenian dragon carpets', but since then, very little text has been devoted to Armenian rugs. The fact that Christianity became the state religion of Armenia in the third century has been overlooked by those who speak of 'Islamic' rugs, thus completely ignoring this rather important group of Christian weavers. Today, the expertise of rug repair and restoration seems to be largely in the skilled hands of Armenians.

ARMENIBAFF *Persian*
The name, meaning 'Armenian knot', is sometimes applied to rugs woven in Armenian villages in the Chahar Mahal region of Iran.

ASGHAND (AZGHAND) *Persian*
See Khorasan.

ASMALYK (OSMULDUK) *Turkoman*
Pentagonal Yomut bag.

ASSADABAD *Persian*
See Hamadan.

ATA
See Yomut.

AT-CHEKI *Turkoman*
Horse girth-band.

AT-JOLI *Turkoman*
Horse blanket.

'AUBUSSON'
During the nineteenth and early twentieth centuries, various rug weaving areas in Persia and the Caucasus copied Aubusson designs either on order, or in an attempt to revitalize the flagging rug trade.

Aubusson is a town on the Creuse River in central France. It has been famed for its carpets and tapestries since the fifteenth century.

The term is included here both as an explanation of the occurrence of Aubusson designs in some Oriental rugs, and because the term is sometimes used as a prefix to 'Caucasian' or 'Persian'.

AVANOS *Anatolian*
Modern rugs from the Turkish village of that

58

name, west of Kayseri. See Kayseri.

AVONYA (AVUNYA) *Anatolian*
Pre-1923 name of Ezine, a village south of
Çanakkale. The rugs from the surrounding
area were sometimes sold as Avonya and
sometimes as Bergama. They are of the
Bergama type.

AYATLYK *Turkoman*
Rugs in which the Turkoman carried their
dead to the burial site.

AZERBAIJAN *Iran and U.S.S.R., Map: H4*
This Iranian province used to embrace not
only a large portion of north-western Iran,
but also part of the southern Caucasus which
is now in the U.S.S.R. An Azerbaijan rug is
therefore one from this region which cannot
be more positively identified, and could be a
Karadagh, a Karaje, or one of the Kurdish
weaves.

AZGHAND (ASGHAND) *Persian*
See Khorasan.

BAGSHAISH (BAKSHIS, BAKSHAYESH)
Persian, Map, see Bakshis: G4
Village in the Heriz district which produces
rugs of this name in the Heriz technique. The
oldest-known rugs are not believed to be
more than one hundred and fifty years old.

BAHAR *Persian*
See Hamadan.

BAHARLU *Persian*
Rugs woven by the Baharlu, one of the tribes

of the Khamseh Confederation in the Shiraz
area of the Fars province. See Khamseh
Confederation and Niriz.

BAKHTIARI (BAKHTYAR) *Persian, Map: H7*
At least two distinct weave patterns fall under
this heading. One is that of the Bakhtiari
tribe who have for a long time led a
semi-nomadic life in the Zagros Mountains
between Kharramabad in the north and
Soleyman in the south. The others come from
the Chahar Mahal region where a number of
villages inhabited by various ethnic groups
make rugs in designs that are traditionally
Bakhtiari. These latter rugs are sold as
Bakhtiari even though they are not made by
this tribe.
    Edwards says that the term as applied to
rugs 'is a misnomer; for the so-called
Bakhtiaris are not woven by Bakhtiari tribes
at all'.[11] He was referring to the rugs from the
Chahar Mahal region, and, in so far as his
assertion refers to those, we agree with his
comment. It is to be noted, however, that
Austen Henry Layard, the eminent British
archaeologist who discovered the ruins of
Nineveh in the mid nineteenth century, lived
among a group of Bakhtiari for some time,
and in his notes he described the beautiful
rugs, woven by the women, in designs that
were handed down from mother to daughter.
He was so impressed by the rugs of the
Bakhtiari that he tried to arrange for their
export to Western markets.[12]
    The name 'Bibibaff' is often used to
describe the best quality Bakhtiari rugs. The
term is used among the Qashqa'i with the
same connotation. The exact derivation of the
term is not clear, but 'bibi' means 'first wife'

59

and 'baff' means 'knot'. See Bibibaff.

The rugs from the Chahar Mahal region are also sold under the names of the villages where they were made. Among the better-known ones are Chalchotor, Saman, Shalengar, Kafero and Khorey. Other names will undoubtedly come into prominence as the products of different villages find favour in Western markets.

BAKRA *Indian*
Modern rug.

BAKSHIS *Persian, Map: G4*
See Bagshaish.

BAKU *Caucasian, Map: H4, Plates 3, 4*
Oil has built this city into the fifth largest of the U.S.S.R. Situated on the southern side of the Apsheron Peninsula, it is the capital of the Azerbaijan Soviet Socialist Republic.

In the twelfth century it was the capital of the Shahs of Shirvan and therefore, strictly on a geographical basis, the rugs of Baku should be included among the Shirvan group. On a design and colour basis, there is merit in separating them from the so-called 'Shirvans', but not on the basis of their weave pattern.

Schürmann subdivides the Bakus into Boteh-Chila, Chila, Surahani and Saliani.[13] Another design subdivision frequently referred to by other authorities is Afshan-Chila.

BALIKESIR (BALIKESHIR) *Anatolian*
Capital of the province of the same name situated about ninety kilometres north-east of Bergama. Rugs sold under this name are usually the products of the nearby Karakeçili tribe. The town of Balikesir itself produces rugs which may be sold as Bergama, Balikesir or Kirshehir.

BALISHT *Afghanistan*
O'Bannon[14] says that this word is synonymous with 'torba' meaning 'a donkey bag'; both terms are used in Afghanistan but 'torba' is more common in the north and 'balisht' more common in the south.

BALKAN
Rugs of this name come from Bosnia, Bulgaria, Yugoslavia and Romania. The craft was introduced into these countries at the time of the Turkish occupation.

BALUCHI *Map: K5, L8, N8*
See Belouch.

BALVARDI *Persian*
See Afshar.

BAM *Persian*
Coarsely knotted rugs from the city of Bampur in south-eastern Iran.

BANDHOR *Anatolian*
'An anecdote illustrative of the way in which new rug-names are secured is told by Mr. W.H. Banta. It relates to the Bandhor rugs, which are known far and wide throughout this country as a heavy and rather low-priced quality of Asia Minor carpets. "Many years ago", he said, "there was ordered by a New York firm a line of stout carpets on the model of the modern Ghiordes, but with some variation in design. When the first one

60

arrived a gentleman from Boston saw it, liked it, and offered right away to buy it. A price was named, double what we had really intended to sell it at, but he didn't baulk. When he asked the name of the fabric we had no name to give him, so two or three of us got out a map of the East, and each selected a name. These, written on slips of paper, were placed in a hat, and I put in my hand and drew out the paper bearing the word Bandhor. So we called the rug Bandhor, and they have been so known ever since.'' '
(John Kimberly Mumford, *Oriental Rugs;*
4 ed., p. 6)

The anecdote is possibly a unique example of name fabrication, but in the vernacular of the rug world there are a number of names that are equally meaningless.

BANJALUKA *Balkan*
According to Jacoby,[15] this is the name given to embroidered carpets from the Balkans. The city of Banjaluka is in northern Bosnia, Yugoslavia.

BARIK *Persian*
See Hamadan.

BASHADAR *Map: S1*
The oldest-known fragment of a knotted rug dating from between the third and sixth centuries B.C. was found at Bashadar in the Altai Mountains of Central Asia. See Pazyryk.

BASHERI *Turkoman*
See Afghan.

BASIRI *Persian*
See Khamseh Confederation.

BASRA *Anatolian*
See Ghiordes.

BAYASID *Persian*
Town situated in north-western Iran near the Turkish frontier. Although recognized as a collecting point for Kurdish rugs, it has no standing as a rug description, although it has been used as such.

BECTASH *Anatolian*
The Textile Museum, Washington, D.C., has two rugs of this name. They are undoubtedly Turkish but no additional information regarding their provenance has been established. The name may have some connection with the Bektaşi order of dervishes founded by the legendary Haci (Hajji) Bektaş. Even if it does, the link takes the matter no further and does not tell us where the rugs were made, because at the end of the nineteenth century and the beginning of the twentieth, the order had lodges all over the Ottoman Empire in close proximity to one another.

BEHBEHAN *Persian*
Rugs with motifs similar to those of the Qashqa'i but woven by Lur tribes in the Fars area. See Gabeh and Lurs.

BEILLERI *Persian*
See Afshar.

BELOUCH (BALUCHI) *Map, see Baluchi: K5, L8, N8, Plates 5, 6*
The Baluchi people, like the Kurds, speak a west-Iranian language, which supports the belief that they migrated from regions near

61

the Caspian Sea to the areas which they now inhabit. Today they are to be found in groups in Pakistan, Afghanistan, southern Soviet Central Asia and in the Khorasan province of Iran.

The spelling of 'Baluchi to describe the people is that of the National Geographic Society, but the rugs are more commonly known by the form 'Belouch', though the present generation of students are using the form 'Baluchi' to describe the rugs as well.

Their rugs display colour and structural features that are more akin to Turkoman weaves than any other group, yet design-borrowings from the Caucasus and Persia are apparent. Contemporary students believe that the Baluchi did once have a gul that they could call their own, and there are design features that are exclusively Belouch. But, as Noel Hobbs points out, although their designs are multifarious and frequently copies of designs from other areas, 'the stamp of the Baluchi is seen, not only in the weaving itself, but in the use of colour and often lustrous wool quality'.[16]

Dr Dietrich H.G. Wegner, when addressing the International Conference on Oriental Carpets – held in London during June 1976 – on the rugs of the Baluchi, pointed out that to an extent Belouch designs can be attributed to various areas of origin. At this stage we cannot yet say whether regional attributions are possible on the basis of differing weave patterns. The problem of specific attribution is further complicated by the products of the Timuri who, although ethnically distinct from the Baluchi, weave rugs in the Belouch style.

Three names have been used for grades of Belouch rugs from Khorasan: 'Meshed' for the best, 'Kuduani' for the medium, and 'Arab' for the poorest quality. The term 'Arab Belouch' also refers to rugs from the Firdaus area of Khorasan which is inhabited largely by Arabs who make rugs in the Belouch style.

Plate 6 shows an antique Belouch from Khorasan with a not uncommon Belouch version of a Persian design, known as the Mina Khani. The weave of this rug should dispel the fallacy that the Baluchi are incapable of excellent work.

Very good Belouch rugs were also produced in Afghanistan, a number of them from south of Herat.

The term 'Baluchistan' or 'Belouchistan' is sometimes used for the rugs made by the Baluchi people, but this is misleading as a very small proportion of Belouch rugs are made in Baluchistan. See Adraskand, Sistan and Siyar-kar.

BERDELIK *Anatolian*
Turkish term for door or wall hangings.

BERGAMA *Anatolian, Map: A3*
Name applied to the rustic rugs which come from a large area to the north and east of the ancient city of Pergamon or Pergamum, a name that was changed by Atatürk to Bergama. Rugs made in the following villages are recognized as belonging to the Bergama group: Akhisar, Manyas, Yuntdag, Avonya (Ezine), Balikesir, Çanakkale (near the ancient city of Troy), Soma and Yaçebedir. The Yaçebedirs have been referred to as 'charcoal carpets' because of their dark colouring.

In addition to the products of the rural

communities around Bergama, manufactories have existed there from a very early date, probably the fourteenth century, and rugs are believed to have come from this area as early as the thirteenth century. Bergama was one of the main centres of Ottoman carpet production and some of the so-called 'Holbeins' – the type depicted in the painting *The Ambassadors* by Hans Holbein, and dated 1533 – were probably made in the area. See 'Holbein'.

BERGENDEH *Persian*
See Hamadan.

BESHIR (BESHIRE, BASHERI) *Turkoman, Map: M4, Plates 17, 18*
This tribe is often described as 'Ersari Beshir' to underline the accepted belief that they are a subdivision of the Ersari tribe. At an early stage of the Ersari's southward migrations, possibly around the seventeenth century, the Beshir settled on the middle reaches of the Amu Darya within the Khanate of Bokhara, and became largely sedentary. As a sedentary people they were more exposed to outside influence, which explains their design features and use of colour which is often distinct from the other Ersari. Many of their weavings show the influence of Persia and East Turkestan in design though their character remains completely individual. The weave pattern of these rugs clearly shows their Ersari affiliation. See Bokhara, Ersari and Afghan.

BHARISTAN *Indian*
Dilley[17] reported that the manufactories of Amritsar in India at one time, probably early

in the twentieth century, used 'Laristan' as a trade name. These same rugs were subsequently sold under various trade names such as 'Bharistan', 'Iranshah' and 'Shahristan' – to add to the confusion.

BIBIBAFF (BIBI BAFT) *Persian*
This term is most commonly applied to the best quality Bakhtiari rugs, but it is also used as a quality description amongst the Qashqa'i.

As a quality description it derives from a twofold assumption, firstly, that the best rugs were made by the most experienced weavers, and secondly, that the 'bibi' (first wife) was the most experienced weaver in the family. The word 'baff' (knot) is found frequently in rug terminology, for example, 'Armenibaff' (made by Armenians), 'Farsibaff' (made with the Fars, Persian, Senneh or open knot), and 'Turkibaff' (made with the closed or Turkish knot).

BIBIKABAD (BUBUKABAD) *Persian*
See Hamadan.

BIJAR (BIDJAR) *Persian, Map: G5, Plates 7, 8*
The town of this name is in Persian Kurdistan, but the Bijar rugs are very different from other Kurdish work.

They are very heavy in relation to their size, and sometimes impossible to fold, the explanation for which lies in the knotting technique: one of the two warps surrounded by each knot is directly under the other and the weft is beaten down to make a very compact fabric, as robust as any rug is ever likely to be.

According to Mumford,[18] dealers in the

Western world at one time called Bijars 'Saraks', a corruption of 'Serakhs', the oasis (Map: L5) from where it was believed, in some circles, that the Bijar weavers came at the time of Genghis and Timur. The belief and the name have both been discarded.

BIDJOV (BIDSHOFF) *Caucasian, Map: H3*
Design classification of rugs from the Shirvan area. According to Hubel,[19] these rugs came from the Caucasian town of Akhssu (not to be confused with Aksu in Central Asia).

BIJAPUR *Indian*
City in southern India which used to produce rugs that were sold in Western markets; but production appears to have ceased, or possibly they are now sold under some other name.

BILOOZ
Early spelling of the word 'Belouch'.

BILVERDI *Persian*
Modern rug from the village of the same name in the Heriz area of Azerbaijan.

BIRJAND (BIRCHEND, BIRDSHEND, BIRJEND, BIREDCHEND) *Persian, Map: K7*
The spelling of 'Birjand' is that used by the National Geographic Society for the town of that name in the province of Khorasan. This name usually denotes the poorest quality of Khorasan work.

BOKCHE (BOKTSCHE) *Turkoman*
Small square kelim with four triangular knotted pieces attached one to each edge and which fold inwards to form a bag.

BOKHARA (BUKHARA) *Turkestan, Map, see Bukhara: M4*
According to Barthold, Hartley Clark and the *Encyclopaedia Britannica*, the common Central Asian pronunciation is *Bukhărā*. Known as Sogdiana at the time of Alexander the Great, it appears to have acquired its present name after the Arab conquests in A.D. 640.

At one time it was the capital of the Khanate of Bokhara, which included Khiva, Meshed and Herat. For centuries it was a seat of Islamic learning and until recent times the principal book market of Central Asia. A city of such importance was without doubt a market of equal importance where the local weavers as well as others from further afield sold their rugs.

It was for this reason, and the fact that early students were unable to provide a more accurate identity, that all Turkoman products were, and unfortunately sometimes still are, called 'Bokhara'. There is, however, no acceptable evidence that rugs of a technique or design distinctive from any of the products of the main Turkoman weaving tribes, namely, the Salor, Tekke, Yomut, Saryk or Ersari, were made here, and therefore, the continued use of the name merely blurs more appropriate identification.

Attempts have been made to label what would now be called a 'Beshir' as the true Bokhara. In support of the argument, it is pointed out that the Beshir designs are distinctive, and the Beshir lived in the Khanate of Bokhara. The opposing argument is that all the other tribes have distinctive designs, and all the main tribes were to be found in the Khanate at one time or another.

Rugs were probably woven in Bokhara

which was renowned for various textiles – including embroideries and the intricate Ikat work – which required not only the stability of a sedentary existence, but the presence of an opulent market. However, it cannot be assumed that any particular tribe or group held the weaving monopoly within the town walls. No doubt the carpets of every weaving tribe were sold at one time or another on the Bokhara market.

The term 'Russian Bokhara' is one that has crept into rug terminology to distinguish between a Turkoman rug from Central Asia, made since the advent of the Russians, and the Turkoman derivatives and Turkoman rugs made in and around Gurgan in north-eastern Iran.

Under the subheading 'Nomenclature' we have mentioned the unknown derivation and unjustified usage of the names 'Princess' and 'Royal' Bokhara for two types of rug made by the Tekke tribe. One also finds the various Turkoman tribe names prefixed to Bokhara as in 'Tekke Bokhara'. This usage is also unjustified because there are no structural or design features peculiar to the city or Khanate of Bokhara.

BOKHARA STRIPS
See Kibitka.

BOLESH-MOTAKA *Turkoman*
According to Hubel[20] this is a name for a small cushion.

BOR *Anatolian*
The only author who appears to have mentioned rugs of this name is Hubel.[21] He says, 'In Bor near Nigde there was a Greek school of knotting which went on into the twentieth century. They imitated mainly Ladik, Ghiordes and Kula prayer rugs. The rugs all have the name Bor and a number knotted into the upper end.' Modern rugs made in Bor are more often sold as Nigde.

BORDCHELU (BORDSHALY, BORCHALOU, BOZCHELU, BURJALU) *Persian*
See Hamadan.

BORDJALOU *Caucasian, Map: G3*
See Kazak.

BORLOU *Anatolian*
Modern type of rug from the Smyrna area.

BORUJIRD *Persian, Map, see Borujerd: H6*
See Burujird.

BOTEH-CHILA *Caucasian*
See Baku.

BOU
Turkoman word for tent bands. See Kibitka.

'BRAGANÇA' *Indian*
The small group known as the 'Bragança carpets' takes its name from the Bragança Palace in Lisbon where the type was first recognized. They were made in India during the seventeenth or early eighteenth centuries and because of their unusual square shape, are believed to have been designed for Western markets. Their shape distinguishes them as a subdivision of the larger group of Indo-Persian carpets of the same period. One example is to be seen at Boughton House, home of the Duke of Buccleugh and

Queensbury, in Warwickshire, England.

BROUSSA *Anatolian, Map, see Bursa: B3*
See Bursa.

BUNYAN *Anatolian*
See Kayseri.

BURDUR *Anatolian*
Capital of the province of the same name in
south-western Turkey, thirty-odd kilometres
west of Isparta. Rugs from here are of the
Isparta type, and are usually sold under that
name.

BURSA *Anatolian, Map: B3*
Osman, the founder of the Ottoman Empire
is buried in Bursa, or Broussa as the town was
formerly called. Bursa was known as a carpet
manufacturing centre as early as the fifteenth
century when its silk carpets and textiles
received wide acclaim. Inferior rugs are made
there today but the town remains one of
Turkey's largest producers of silk.

**BURUJIRD (BURUJERD, BORUJERD,
BORUJIRD)** *Persian, Map, see Borujerd: H6*
West of Sultanabad is the town of Burujird
where a small rug-production is carried on.
The rugs are of the Seraband design but differ
from them in certain structural aspects.

CABISTAN *Caucasian*
See Kabistan.

CAESAREAN *Anatolian*
Mumford[22] mentions this name as one used
for various Anatolian rugs. 'Kayseri' is

derived from this name.

CAIRENE *Egyptian, Map, see Cairo: A7*
Erdmann[23] and others held the view that rug
manufactories were set up in Cairo during
the reign of the Mamluks (1252-1517).
Another view is that the court manufactories
there appeared only after the Ottoman
conquest in 1517, and assert therefore, that
the Mamluk or Cairene rugs of that era should
more properly be classified as Ottoman,
though made in Cairo.[24]

This controversy concerned a group of
carpets which had been known as Damascus
carpets, their conjectural place of origin. The
name was superseded by the term 'Cairene'
following Frederick Sarre's persuasive
argument propounded in the early 1920s that
their most probable origin was Egypt.[25] See
Damascus and Mamluk.

ÇAL *Anatolian*
This town, south of Ushak, produces a small
number of rugs which are sold under this
name. Rugs made in the neighbouring village
of Zeyve are also sold as Çal or Isparta.

ÇAN *Anatolian*
West Anatolian village rug.

ÇANAKKALE *Anatolian, Map: A2*
Capital of the province of the same name in
north-western Turkey. The name is derived
from 'çanak', meaning 'pot', and 'kale',
meaning 'fortress'. The town is renowned for
its pottery. As a rug name it belongs to the
Bergama group.

CANAPE *Persian*

See Hamadan.

CARIAN *Anatolian*
Rug that came from the province of Caria. These rugs are now referred to as 'Melaz' which has completely superseded the name 'Carian'.

CAYN (QA'IN) *Persian*
See Khorasan.

CHADIR-SHERIDI *Anatolian*
Turkish name for a tent band or strip.

CHAHAR-RA *Persian*
See Hamadan.

CHAJLI *Caucasian, Map: H4*
See Shirvan.

CHAKISH
See Afghan.

CHALCHOTOR *Persian*
See Bakhtiari.

CHALYK (KALYK, KHALYK) *Turkoman*
See Kalyk.

CHAN-KARABAGH *Caucasian*
See Karabagh.

CHARPAY (TSCHARPAI) *Turkoman*
Dimensional term applied to Afghans. Jacoby gives the derivation of the term as a compound of 'chahaer' and 'pai' meaning 'four foot'.[26]

CHARSHANGHO (CHARSHANGU,

CHARSHANG GHO) *Turkoman, Map, see Charshangu: M5*
In O'Bannon's opinion, 'the Charshangho who made carpets before 1884 were probably a sub-tribe of the Salor living between Penjdeh and Maimana and that, as a result of the many defeats and geographical dislocations to which they were subjected in the nineteenth century, this sub-tribe has been assimilated by the Ersari'.[27]

O'Bannon goes on to show that the structure of these old Charshangho rugs was very similar to that of the Salors. Bogolyubov[28] also places this type within the Salor group, and Schürmann,[29] who illustrates two pieces of similar design, suggests that they were made by Salors living on 'the northern middle reaches of the Amu Darya towards Khiva'. Another similar piece, Item 9a in the carpet study section of the Textile Department of the Victoria and Albert Museum, London, is described by the Museum as 'Ersari' but has a weave pattern clearly identifiable with that of the beautiful Salor fragment in the Museum of Fine Arts, Boston[30] (see Plates 61, 62). See Afghan and Ersari.

CHAUDOR (CHODOR) *Turkoman, Map, see Chodor: J3, K3/L3, Plates 9, 10*
Some authors have described this tribe as an offshoot or subdivision of the Yomut. In so far as historical fact can be extricated from legend, it seems more probable that they were in existence as a separate autonomous group before the Yomut. This contention is supported by the lists of the Oghuz clans provided by Mahmud Kashghari and Rashid al-din, neither of whom mentions the Yomut,

though both mention the 'Juvaldur' and 'Javuldur' respectively. These have been identified as names for the tribe now called the 'Chaudor', or 'Chodor' as it is sometimes spelt.

The quality of weave to be found in Chaudor rugs appears to vary to a greater extent than that of the weaves of any other Turkoman group. These variations may not all be due to differing qualities of the same weave pattern – some may be the work of other tribes. See Yomut for comments on the 'greater Yomut group'.

Plate 10 depicts a Chaudor rug. A rug of very similar design is described by Schürmann as 'Yomut',[31] but as the authors have not seen the weave pattern of that particular rug, no further comment on it can be made.

CHEKH RAJAB *Persian*
Fairly low quality modern Heriz-type rug, woven in the village of the same name, in Azerbaijan.

CHELABERD *Caucasian, Map: G4, Plates 29, 30*
Although the design of these rugs, the so-called 'Eagle Kazaks', shows an affinity to the Kazaks, structurally they are indisputably Karabagh. Compare Plate 29 (Karabagh) and Plate 33 (Kazak). The structural rule of the Karabaghs is two weft threads after every two rows of knots. The Kazaks on the other hand all appear to have an irregular number of wefts, from two to four, after every row of knots. See Karabagh.

CHELIM

See Kelim.

CHELSEA CARPET *Persian*
An early sixteenth-century carpet which hangs in the Victoria and Albert Museum, London. Many feel it to be a work of greater artistic accomplishment than the Ardebil Carpet. Apart from the fact that the Museum purchased it from a dealer in the King's Road, Chelsea – hence its name – there is no other data concerning its history.

CHEMCHE-TORBA *Turkoman*
Variously described as a Turkoman salt bag or horse feeding-bag, but literally a spoon bag.

CHERKESS *Caucasian*
See Tcherkess.

CHERLIK *Turkoman*
Saddle cover.

CHI CHI (TZI TZI) *Caucasian, Map: H3, Plates 11, 12*
This name is believed to be derived from that of the Caucasian tribe, the Chechen, who live on the northern flank of the Greater Caucasus. The Chechens became famous in the nineteenth century for their heroic resistance, under the leadership of Shaykh Shamil of Daghestan, to Russian expansionist operations in the Caucasus. They are now incorporated in the Chechen-Ingush Autonomous Soviet Socialist Republic. The name Chi Chi applies to a very distinctive type of rug design and colour scheme. It is not known whether the rugs were woven exclusively by the tribe from which their name is derived, though it seems unlikely in

that the design is found in association with a number of different weave patterns – the same ones, in fact, that occur throughout the eastern Caucasian rug groups called Baku, Kuba, Daghestan and Shirvan. See Daghestan and Kuba.

CH'IEN LUNG (KEEN-LUND) *Chinese*
See Chinese and Keen-Lund.

CHILA *Caucasian*
See Baku and Hila.

CHINDA *Indian*
Type of Indian manufactory rug of poor quality.

CHINESE
Approaching the study of Chinese rugs requires an almost complete disregard for the precepts of the art applicable elsewhere. The problems presented are manifold. Firstly, with regard to designs, we find that with very few exceptions they were not regionally traditional. They were not only used universally but also faithfully copied, sometimes centuries after the manufacture of the prototype. Furthermore, although designs may have declined in popularity as new ones became acceptable, there was no determinable cessation in the use of one, just as there was no sudden acceptance of another. Secondly, although structural differences exist, these appear to be applications of a universal technique to a particular purpose rather than regional variations. The result of these complexities is that precise provenance is beyond the expert's accomplishment.

Attributing age to a Chinese carpet is correspondingly difficult; as Lorenz says, 'Opinion rather than indisputable evidence assigns them to a certain reign.'[32] The method used by the authorities is that of attributing a carpet to the period of the reigning emperor at the conjectural time of manufacture. The earliest surviving examples of the craft are believed to have been made at the time of Ch'ung Chên, the last emperor of the Ming dynasty, who died in the first half of the seventeenth century. The Ching dynasty succeeded the Ming dynasty and survived until the creation of the Republic in 1912. The emperors of the Ching dynasty were: Shun Chih (1644-1661), K'ang Hsi (1661-1722), Yung Cheng (1723-1735), Ch'ien Lung (1736-1796), Chia Ch'ing (1796-1820), Tao Kuang (1821-1850), Hsien Feng (1851-1861), T'ung Chih (1862-1874), Kuang Hsii (1875-1908), and Hsuang T'ung (1908-1912).

The asymmetrical knot is the one most commonly found in Chinese rugs though the symmetrical is used, but frequently only in side edges. Knot density is low, with generally twenty knots or less to the linear decimetre. In China, artistic expression was more highly esteemed than technical excellence and the result is that some of the most beautiful pieces are found with unusually coarse knotting. In the greater part of the rug weaving world on the other hand, a high value was placed on craftsmanship, and beautiful rugs were generally also very well made.

CHIQCHI *Afghanistan*
See Afghan.

CHOB BASH (CHUBASH) *Afghanistan*
The origin and history of this tribe is not
clear, but it is likely that they have lived in
what is now Afghanistan for more than a
century. Wegner[33] believes that they are an
offshoot of the Chaudor who migrated into
Afghanistan via Pendeh. O'Bannon[34] treats
them as a tribe of the Ersari group and
illustrates what he calls an 'antique Chob
Bash' carpet which clearly has Ersari Afghan
features. Schürmann[35] illustrates a rug which
he calls 'Afghan of the Chob Bash' with
considerable design and colour similarities to
O'Bannon's rug, but it looks less like Ersari
work. Not having seen these rugs we do not
know if they are structurally similar.

   The tribe is an important producer of
modern Afghan rugs. See Afghan.

CHONDZORESK *Caucasian, Map: G4*
These rugs are often called 'cloudband
Kazaks' but according to Schürmann[36] they
are Karabagh. Some Chondzoresks are in
structure without doubt Karabagh, but there
are others indisputably Kazak. We deduce
from this that the same design was used by
two groups of people using different
techniques, and not that different techniques
were used by one group of people.

CHOURDJIN
See Kharjin.

CHOUVAL (CHUVAL)
See Juval.

CHOY *Persian*
See Koy.

CIRCASSIAN *Caucasian*
See Tcherkess.

COBISTAN *Caucasian*
See Kabistan.

DAGHESTAN *Caucasian, Map: G3/H3, Plates
13, 14*
Now a Soviet Socialist Republic in the
north-eastern part of Caucasia. Within the
span of our rug weaving knowledge,
Daghestan has always included three areas
whose names are famous as rug types, Kuba,
Derbend and Daghestan. Schürmann[37]
classifies each of these names as main rug
groups with the following subdivisions:
Lesghi, Seyshour, Konaghend, Perepedil,
Karagashli, Zejwa and other less common
names. The Chi Chi also belong with this
group, though the tribe from which they
derive their name lives to the west of
Daghestan in an area that has at times been
incorporated into Daghestan, but is now an
autonomous republic. See Chi Chi.

   Attributing rugs to any one of the three
groups, Kuba, Derbend and Daghestan, on
the criterion of design, is only acceptable if
one takes the view that designs were not
freely copied. We believe that it is unrealistic
to take such a view. It is also not possible to
designate a weave pattern – or for that matter
any other structural feature – as being the sole
prerogative of any one of these groups.
Although there are structural variations in the
rugs of the overall area, these variations all
appear within each individual group, and can
neither be demarcated geographically, nor by
design association. Whether or not this

70

situation always existed is not known; logic dictates that at some earlier time certain designs must have existed in conjunction with particular weave patterns as was the case in Persia and Turkestan, for example. But a lack of both sufficiently old examples and relevant historical data means that we do not know if those weave patterns were traditional solely to the area where the design arose, or if they were the traditional manner of weaving of a much larger area. In the latter event one can draw an analogy with the Hamadan area where different designs are made in different villages, but the weaving technique is similar over a very large area.

Unravelling the complexities of eastern Caucasian rugs is probably the most difficult and frustrating problem arising in the whole of the rug weaving world. This is not really surprising when one considers that there are over fifty ethnic groups in Caucasia speaking over one hundred and fifty dialects. From antiquity to the seventeenth century there were successive waves of invaders including Scythians, Alans, Huns, Khazars, Arabs, Seljuk Turks and Mongols. Not without reason has it been said that Caucasia is the world's best-stocked linguistic museum – and Daghestan is Caucasia's.

Travelling further south to the Shirvan area we find no clearcut division between the rugs of that area and Daghestan. Whatever criteria one uses – design, weave pattern, selvedges, end structure, colour or materials – sufficient examples will be found with the same features in rugs of both areas to make any attempt at positive identification of no avail.

An examination of the weave patterns of Plates 3, 11, 13 and 71 reveals visible differences. These differences could be used for identification if they were found in consistent association with particular designs, or if they were confined to particular areas in eastern Caucasia. This unfortunately does not appear to be the case.

We do not object to names which refer to particular designs, such as Perepedil, Seyshour or Marasali, as they are the very fabric of the mystique attaching to the enchanting variations of colour and design found in the rugs of Caucasia. It is nevertheless somewhat unfortunate that the enchantment is a little tainted by dogmatic assertions of attributions which imply that various designs are the monopoly of one or another village or area.

DAGHESTANIAN *Caucasian*
See Akty-Mikra.

DALI
See Afghan.

DAMAQ *Persian*
See Hamadan.

'DAMASCUS' *Egyptian*
Von Bode and Kühnel[38] and Erdmann[39] shared the view that the *tapeti damaschini* mentioned in fifteenth and sixteenth-century Venetian inventories referred to a damask-like appearance rather than to rugs themselves as coming from Damascus, which does not seem ever to have produced knotted rugs. The term *tapeti damaschini* was superseded by the term 'Cairene' when it became accepted that the rugs were made in the Cairo workshops during the Mamluk

period. It is quite likely that rugs made in Egypt were sold through Damascus which, in spite of the decline in its fortunes under the Ottomans, continued to trade with Venice. See Cairene.

DARAK-BASH *Turkoman*
Decorative cover for the wool comb, also called dokme-darak.

DARÇEÇLI *Anatolian*
Hubel[40] refers to the Darcecli as a type of Yürük.

DARGAZINE (DERGEZINE, DERYAZIN) *Persian*
See Dergezine and Hamadan.

DARRESHURI *Persian*
See Qashqa'i.

DASHTAB *Persian*
See Afshar.

DAULATABAD *Afghanistan, Map: M5*
See Afghan.

DAULATABAD *Persian*
Village near Hamadan where rugs of the Hamadan class are made. Not to be confused with the Afghan name.

DAVAÇ *Anatolian*
See Konya.

DAZKIRI *Anatolian*
These rugs have been made in the village of that name west of Isparta and south-east of Ushak for at least a century.

DEHAJ *Persian*
See Afshar.

DEH SHOTORAN *Persian*
See Afshar.

DELHI *Indian*
Manufactory rugs were made in Delhi from the seventeenth century, and some modern Indian rugs are still sold under that name.

DEMIRÇI (DEMIRDJI) *Anatolian, Map: B3*
In this town just north of Ghiordes, rug weaving on a commercial scale was an innovation of the late nineteenth century at a time when the demand of Western markets was creating new weaving areas all over the Orient. It is uncertain if weaving of any significance existed here prior to this period, but whatever the situation, the production of Demirçi has never been celebrated for its quantity or quality. Occasionally one hears of a 'Demirçi-Kula' – a name contrived to denote a Demirçi with Kula design features. If such a contrivance were allowed to develop to its ultimate nonsensical conclusion, a hyphenated string of who knows how many names would also be acceptable. See Kula and Hindustanieh.

DENIZLI *Anatolian*
See Isparta.

DERBEND (DERBENT) *Caucasian, Map, see Derbent: H3*
If the structure is coarser, if the design is cruder, if the colours are duller, if its existence is defenceless, in fact, if it is inferior – it must be a Derbend! That is a fair

summation of the universal reaction to Derbends manufactured over the last hundred years. During the twentieth century the Russians had great difficulty overcoming Western sales resistance to the name, a problem which they attempted to resolve by substituting the name Akty-Mikra for the products previously offered as Derbends.

Some authors maintain that Derbends were not always inferior products. For our part, we wonder whether the name ever had any structural or design significance which set the rugs apart from the other rugs of Daghestan. Hawley said that 'those that are ordinarily found in the market are like poor imitations of inferior Daghestans'.[41] We suggest that Derbend, an ancient and important seaport on the Caspian, lent its name to products from the interior which did not conform with the features which early rug dealers, rightly or wrongly, came to accept as Daghestan. Schürmann says that 'the multiplicity of the design motifs, which are taken from Kuba, Shirvan and Daghestan, allow of no distinguishing features for Derbends'.[42] See Daghestan.

DERBENT *Anatolian*
Rug weaving village near Konya in west-central Turkey, not to be confused with the Caucasian Derbend. Rugs from here are more likely to be sold as Konya.

DERGEZINE (DARGAZINE, DERYAZIN) *Persian*
Rugs from a village of this name and its surrounding area some sixty kilometres north of Hamadan.

DIAH DIZLUK *Turkoman*
Small knotted pieces used to decorate the knees of the camel or horse used in the wedding procession.

DIP KHALI *Turkoman*
Term for the small threshold carpet used in a tent.

DIS TORBA *Turkoman*
Word for a small bag used to store salt or other foodstuffs such as flour or tea.

DJIDJIM (JINJIN)
The name is applied to various flatweaves but there is no consensus of opinion as to what the term actually includes. Landreau and Pickering discuss the various usages and conclude that 'if the term djidjim is at all usable, it applies then to portieres and hangings, although it is not altogether clear whether these must be made of strips, especially strips of any particular width, sewn together. Nor is it evident that the term indicates any particular source, or any particular type of weaving.'[43]

DJOUSHEGAN *Persian*
See Joshagan.

DOÇEMEALTI (DOSEMEALTI) *Anatolia, Map, see Dosemealti: B4*
Old weaving area renowned for its rugs of individual design. Those woven in Doçemealti itself are the ones to which the name is validly applied. The surrounding area is inhabited by Yürüks and Kurds whose products are also sometimes labelled Doçemealti because they were marketed

there. See Antalya.

DOROSCH (DOROKHSH, DARAKSH)
Persian
See Khorasan.

DORUYE *Persian*
See Druya.

DOSHAK *Persian*
According to Hubel,[44] a Kurdish word for a large bag or pillow.

DOWLATABAD
See Daulatabad.

DOZAR *Persian*
Dimensional term for a size roughly 183 cm by 122 cm (6ft by 4ft).

'DRAGON KUBA' *Caucasian*
These were at one time known as 'Armenian dragon carpets' and are the earliest surviving Caucasian weaves. Opinion differs on their dating, some authorities placing them as early as the thirteenth century, others – such as Dimand[45] – no earlier than the sixteenth century. Their precise derivation is also problematical. Charles Grant Ellis[46] has made a studious technical analysis of the structure of these carpets but in his text he does not attribute them to any precise area, although during a discussion he expressed the belief that they came from the Caucasus – possibly the Karabagh area – and eastern Anatolia. Whether or not Armenians were involved in their manufacture is not known for certain, but it does seem likely. See Armenian.

DRUYA (DORUYE) *Persian*
Rare reversible rugs from north-western Iran. The knot rows are tied alternately on the two sides of the rug. The name is derived from two words – 'do' meaning 'two', and 'ruya' meaning 'face'.

'EAGLE KAZAK' *Caucasian*
See Chelaberd.

EKBATAN, (EKBATANA, ECBATANA) *Persian*
See Hamadan.

ELLORE *Indian*
A long-established rug weaving centre in southern India where the craft was introduced probably by a group of Persians who settled there some centuries ago. The old rugs were of good quality, but those of this century are mostly, if not all, of inferior quality.

ELVAND (ALVAND) *Persian*
See Hamadan.

ENGSI (ENSI) *Turkoman*
The word for a door-hanging. The Afghan equivalent is 'pardah'. The Armenian word 'hatchli' or 'hatchlou', meaning 'cross', is often used for these pieces. See Hatchli and Pardah. Plates 67 and 68 illustrate an engsi made by the Saryk tribe.

ENILE *Anatolian*
See Inely and Ushak.

ERIVAN *Caucasian, Map, see Yerevan: G3*
Carpets of this name are of relatively recent

74

manufacture. Their name derives from Yerevan, capital of the Armenian Soviet Socialist Republic. They are a commercial creation of the late nineteenth century, and are now more commonly called Yerevan. They have also been called 'Modern Shirvans' or 'Russian Caucasians'.

ERSARI *Turkoman, Map: M6/N6, M5/N5*
Plates 15, 16, 17, 18
According to some authorities, the Ersari tribe includes the Beshir, Charshango and Kizil Ayak as subdivisions; others argue that the Charshango were a Salor subtribe assimilated by the Ersari group near whom they lived in the north-eastern part of present-day Afghanistan; and yet others say that the Kizil Ayak should not be included among the Ersari.

It is clear that the Ersari began moving into the region, now forming part of north-eastern Afghanistan, from as early as the seventeenth century. They were followed by other Turkoman groups, all of whom continued their weaving craft in their new habitat. It is also clear that prior to the twentieth century all the rugs emanating from Afghanistan were made by Turkomans or Baluchi, and not by Afghans, and therefore they would be more appropriately labelled 'Ersari Afghan' or 'Saryk Afghan', rather than simply 'Afghan'.

We have seen a number of rugs identified as Ersari which admittedly include some design features that could be attributed to these versatile weavers. But their weave pattern does not remotely resemble the work of the Ersari, or any other known group of Turkoman weavers. We believe that rugs of this order are classified expediently but incorrectly and suggest that it may even be incorrect to call some of them Turkoman. We refer in that regard to our comments under the entry 'Uzbek' and also suggest that there are surviving examples of the work of Central Asian peoples – Turkoman, Kirghiz, Uzbek, and others – whose identity has been lost by assimilation, or by the insignificance of their numbers or production. See Afghan, Korki and Khiva.

ESKI KERMAN *Persian*
Turkish trade name meaning 'Old Kerman'. See Kerman.

ESKISHEHIR (ESKİŞEHIR) *Anatolian, Map: B3*
Eskişehir is the capital of the western Turkish province of the same name, and has been a rug weaving centre for well over a hundred years. The weavers used to produce an indigenous type of rug, particularly prayer rugs, but later they appear to have practically stopped weaving these when they started to copy Persian and Chinese work. This town is nowadays a large producer of inferior rugs which are often sold under the name of 'Smyrna'.

EVERU *Persian*
See Hamadan.

EYERLIK *Turkoman*
Saddle cover.

EZINE *Anatolian, Map: A3*
This village was called Avunya until 1923 when many of the old Greek names were Turkicized by Atatürk. Rugs made there

before 1923 are still known as Avunya, and those made since are called Ezine.

FACHRALO *Caucasian, Map: G3*
These rugs are in the Kazak group from the point of view both of structure and design, but they tend to be somewhat more finely knotted and shorter piled than most Kazaks. See Kazak.

FAMININ *Persian*
Village rug from the Hamadan area. See Hamadan.

FARSIBAFF *Persian*
The word means 'the knot of Fars', but is applied mainly to those rugs from the Meshed area that are made with the 'jufti' Persian knot. This means that the knots are tied to four instead of two warp threads, resulting in a poorer quality of product. See Khorasan, Turkibaff and Tiebaff.

FARSIMADAN *Persian*
See Qashqa'i

FARSISTAN *Persian*
One of the many names applied to rugs from the Shiraz area, which is in the province of Fars.

FARUKH
See Afghan.

FATEHPUR *Indian*
Two well-known towns, Fatehpur and Fatehpur-Sikri, have a history of rug knotting. Fatehpur-Sikri, thirty-seven kilometres west of Agra (Map: R9) was the first capital of the Mughal Emperor Akbar (1556-1605). After only a few years a shortage of water forced the Emperor to move his capital to Agra. It seems very possible that the earliest Mughal carpets were in fact the products of Fatehpur-Sikri. Having been abandoned it was never reoccupied and remains today a splendid though ruined memorial to Mughal architecture.

The Fatehpur marked on our map (S9) has a history at least as long as Fatehpur-Sikri. Manufactory rugs have come from there for some time but it is not known when the knotting craft was introduced there.

FERAGHAN *Persian, Map: H6, Plates 19, 20*
The renowned rugs of Feraghan were made for a period of roughly one hundred years starting from the middle of the eighteenth century. Their design was generally a refined and unique interpretation of the Herati pattern. This may explain the widely held belief that weavers from Herat were settled in the Feraghan district after Nadir Qoli Beg's conquest of that city in 1732. Nadir Qoli Beg was the man who ascended the throne of Persia in 1736 as Nadir Shah.

The name 'Feraghan' may also refer to a commercial creation of the late nineteenth or early twentieth century with the classical Feraghan design but made in the Sultanabad area. These rugs were generally called Mahals, a name that now signifies a medium quality rug from this area – irrespective of design.

The plates illustrate an antique Feraghan.

FERTEK *Anatolian*

76

Central Anatolian village rugs, usually sold as Nigde.

FESHANE *Anatolian*
According to Turkhan,[47] Feshane was founded as a royal factory in the nineteenth century by Sultan Abdul Medjid [I] (1839-1861), in the Eyub district of Istanbul. Its products were large carpets of Aubusson and Savonnerie designs, and were popular with the Turkish and Egyptian nobility. Feshane was also mentioned by Jacoby[48] but he dates the factory to the time of Sultan Abdul Hamid [II] (1876-1909). The factory today produces cloth in place of carpets.

FETHIYE *Anatolian, Map: A4*
Since 1923 this has been the modern name of Makri (also known as Megri), and the rugs made there since that date are known as Fethiye. See Makri.

FIKIE (AL-FAKIHAH, FIKEH) *Lebanese*
Type of rug which copies Turkish designs and which dates from the period when the area was under Turkish domination.

FINDIGHAN *Caucasian*
Trade name at one time used in Istanbul for a type of rug with a specific design from the eastern Caucasus. These rugs would probably be termed 'Shirvan' or 'Daghestan' by Western dealers. The name is a design description, 'findigh' meaning 'hazelnut'. According to Albrecht Hopf, whose book contains an illustration of a Findighan, they come from 'primitive Daghestan'.[49]

FIRDAUS *Persian*

This name may very occasionally be found on a rug label and it would then signify an Arab Belouch rug made in the area around Firdaus in north-eastern Khorasan. See Belouch.

GABEH (GABA) *Persian*
Name used to describe long-piled rugs of undyed black, brown, grey and cream-coloured wool from the Shiraz area and elsewhere in Iran, but especially from Behbehan, which is in the part of Fars inhabited by the Darreshuri tribe of the Qashqa'i.

GABYSTAN *Caucasian*
See Kabistan.

GAHYN *Persian*
See Qa'in and Khorasan.

GALTUK *Persian*
Rug made in north-western Persia. See Koltuk.

GARUS *Persian*
See Gerous.

GASHGAI *Persian*
See Qashqa'i.

GASHYA *Persian*
See Rupalani.

GASVIN *Persian*
See Kasvin.

GENDJE (GANDJE) *Caucasian, Map, see Kirovabad: G3, Dust-jacket illustration*

Early authors including Mumford[50] and Hawley[51] mention rugs under the names of Genghis, Guendjis, Gengha and Gandje. All of these names are derived from Gengha, the name of a town that was changed to Elizabethpol and then to its present name, Kirovabad. The popular belief is that the town was originally named after Genghis Khan.

An analysis of the descriptions provided by these early authors indicates that they were not referring to one type of rug but to a variety, including Kurdish and Yürük work. The explanation lies in the fact that Gengha was the marketing centre for rugs from the surrounding areas which must have included rugs of varying ethnic origin and of differing designs and structure. Although increased knowledge of the Caucasian rugs has to some extent done away with the custom of naming rugs after the town in which they were marketed, the name 'Gendje' persists, and, we believe, with some justification. There are so-called 'Gendje' rugs which could be more appropriately named. Apart from them, the evidence appears to indicate a separate class, distinctive by weave pattern, that can validly be called Gendje. We base this tentative opinion on the fact that some of the so-called 'Gendjes' have a weave pattern which is different from that of the Kazak, Talish, Moghan, Karabagh and Kurdish rugs. For the present it cannot be said if that group was made by a separate ethnic group or was simply confined to a particular locality. Schürmann[52] allocates a separate class to the rugs of the Gendje district. Samuch-Gendje is a design subdivision of this group.

GENGHA *Caucasian*
See Gendje.

GENGHIS *Caucasian*
See Gendje.

GEORGIAN *Caucasian, Map: G3*
There is no distinctive Georgian rug. This name, like Kutais and Tiflis, originated, as in so many cases, from the town or area where the rugs were purchased. 'Georgian' and 'Kutais' appear to have disappeared from use, but 'Tiflis' is still used by some of the doyens of the trade for rugs that would nowadays more generally, but not necessarily more accurately, be described as Kazak.

GEROUS (GARUS) *Persian*
Bijar is the capital of this district in north-western Iran. The name Gerous is seldom applied to rugs, but when it is, one would understand it to mean the Kurdish weaves from the area, other than the renowned and distinctive Bijars.

Some 'garden' and 'arabesque' carpets of the seventeenth and eighteenth centuries were probably made by Kurds in or around Gerous.

GHALI (QALI, KALI, KHALI) *Persian*
Persian word for a carpet.

GHILIM
See Kelim.

GHIORDES (GÖRDES) *Anatolian, Map: A3, Plates 21, 22*
Rugs of this name do not come from Gordium, the town where Alexander cut the

Ghordian knot, but from Gördes, which is a good three hundred kilometres west of it.

Ghiordes are best known as prayer rugs though other designs and sizes are found, albeit rarely. The Kis-Ghiordes, or so-called 'wedding carpets' ('kis' meaning 'bride'), were made by girls to be given to their husbands on their wedding day. Other design subdivisions of Ghiordes rugs are Basra, Medjidieh, Sineklis and Kara Osman Ghiordes.

The seventeenth and eighteenth-century products of Ghiordes were widely acclaimed as the most beautiful and refined expression of the Turkish rug craft. The extent of their popularity was such that a Panderma manufactory devoted its major effort to copying the masterpieces, ageing them, and passing them off as authentic old Ghiordes rugs.

GILLIM
See Kelim.

GIRDLERS' CARPET *Indian*
Probably the most renowned Mughal carpet. The reason for this is that not only does the central field bear the arms of the Girdlers' Company, in whose hall in London it hangs, and those of the donor, Sir Robert Bell, but also because no other carpet of the same period has as well-recorded a history. Among other documented facts are the date when it was ordered – 1630, the date when it was shipped from India – 1633, and the date when it was presented to the Girdlers' Company – 1634.

GOKLAN *Turkoman*

This tribe was powerful in the seventeenth and eighteenth centuries, but was split in two by the war between Iran and Khiva, and decimated in their battles with the Yomut. They also suffered economically from the growing might of the Tekke. By the nineteenth century they were reduced to two impoverished groups, one on the Gorgan River in Iran and the other in the Khanate of Khiva. Very few rugs are known to have been woven by the Goklan and most of these are flatweaves. According to Bogolyubov,[53] they made only flatweaves of rather coarse quality. But this is possibly another case of over-simplification in the attribution of Turkoman rugs. Although it is speculation to say so at the moment, more systematic research may yet reveal a small and, because of the tribe's poverty, probably not very significant group of rugs made by the Goklan. See Yomut.

GOLDEN AFGHAN *Afghanistan*
By a process of chemical washing, some modern Afghans are bleached to a colour that is intended to emulate the beautiful soft golden shade which age lent to some of the old Ersari Afghans. The colour resemblance is remote and the process so damages the wool that the life expectancy of the rugs is significantly reduced.

GORADIS (GORADIZ) *Caucasian, Map, see Goradiz: H4*
See Karabagh.

GOREVAN (GEORGAVAN) *Persian, Map: G4*
One of the group of villages in north-western Iran which together comprise the

Heriz weaving area. Gorevan has come to be used as a quality description for the most inferior rugs from the Heriz area. See Heriz.

GOUM *Persian*
See Qum.

GOZENE
Hawley[54] is the only author who mentions rugs by this name. It is not clear from his description whether they are Turkish or Persian, but they seem to be of Kurdish or other tribal manufacture. Neither this name, which is probably a poor transliteration, nor anything similar is heard nowadays. It is probably the same as Mumford's Kozan.

GUENDJIS *Caucasian*
See Gendje.

GULISTAN *Persian*
Rugs of this name were made not far from Kashan during the nineteenth century. It is also the name of a type of Ushak made at the beginning of the twentieth century.

GUMBAT (KOUMAT, KOUMBAT) *Persian*
See Hamadan.

GÜNEY *Anatolian*
West Anatolian village which produces rugs sold under the same name.

HAJJI JALIL *Persian*
See Tabriz.

HAMADAN *Persian, Map: H6, Plates 23, 24*

The city of Hamadan (formerly Ecbatana) has a history which dates from pre-biblical times. It was once the capital of Darius the Great, and was the Seljuk capital for fifty years.

Although rug weaving in the city itself is a twentieth-century innovation, Hamadan is the commercial hub of a large rug weaving area that comprises well over seven hundred villages, some of which have been producing rugs for centuries. The vast majority of rugs from this area are woven with a single-wefted technique which produces a distinctive weave pattern which can be seen in Plate 23.

Other types of rugs were made in the area, rugs such as the antique Sarouk, Feraghan, Seraband, Joshagan and Zel-i-Sultan. These have distinctive weaves which can in no way be confused with the Hamadan group.

It is impossible to list all the rug weaving villages in the Hamadan area but the following list comprises the better-known ones, some of which are trade names: Ainabad, Alvand (Elvand), Amsagird, Assadabad, Bahar, Barik, Bergendeh, Bibikabad, Bordchelu (not to be confused with the Caucasian name, Bordjalou), Canape, Chahar-Ra, Damaq, Dargazine, Daulatabad, Ekbatan, Everu, Faminin, Galtuk, Gumbat, Husainabad, Imamzadeh, Injelas, Jechaneh, Joraghan, Jozan, Kabutarahang, Kalajuk, Kara Guez, Kasvin (name used for Alvand rugs), Kerdar, Khamseh (district, not to be confused with the Khamseh Confederation in Fars), Mazlaghan, Mehriban, Melayer (some Melayers do not fall into the Hamadan weave class), Mesrobian, Nobaran, Rahaty, Sard Rud, Saveh (district), Sefiabad, Shahrbaff, Tachtekabi, Tafrish, Tuisserkhan.

HAMMAMLIK *Anatolian*
Bath rug.

HARUN (HAROON) *Persian*
According to Hubel[55] the name signifies
carelessly worked Kashans. Fokker[56] says the
name is that of a village whose products are
sold as 'Haruni-Kashan'. The name first
appeared in the rug trade in the early
twentieth century.

HATCHLI (HATCHLOU, KATCHLI)
Armenian word meaning a 'cross',
misleadingly used in the West to describe
Turkoman tent door-hangings which usually
have a cross-shaped central design motif. It is
very unlikely that this motif has anything to
do with a cross. Far more convincing is the
assertion that the total design, which
includes a frame round the cross shape,
represents a wooden door. See Engsi and
Pardah.

HEHBEHLIK
This word and also 'hehbeh' (which appears
to be an alternative version) are used to
describe a saddle bag. The use of the words
seems to be confined to Turkey and Iran.

HERAT *Persian, now Afghanistan, Map: L6*
City situated in the Harirud Valley, the most
fertile area in Afghanistan. The presence of
water, the climate and the fertility of the soil
have ensured its significance for many
centuries. It attained the peak of its cultural
importance during the reign of the Timurid
Shah Rukh (1405-1447), not solely because of
the Shah – enlightened ruler though he was –
but also because of his vizier son, Baisunqur

Mirza, who established a library and an
academy to promote the arts of the book.

Dimand says that the manufacture of rugs
must have been highly developed at the time
of Shah Rukh and suggests that it was the
designers of Herat and the influence of the
arts of the book that 'were responsible for the
striking changes that were to be seen in the
Safavid rugs of the sixteenth and seventeenth
centuries'.[57] It has also been suggested that
the great Isfahan rugs of the same period
were actually made in Herat.

The Herat rugs of the Persian genre ceased
to be made in the late eighteenth or early
nineteenth century. Today Afghan rugs are
made in Herat and its environs.

HEREKE (HEREK-KEUI) *Anatolian*
A court manufactory was set up in 1844 in
the Gulf of Nicodemia – today known as the
Gulf of Izmit – about sixty-five kilometres
east of Istanbul. Kerman weavers were
imported to train the local people and it is not
surprising, therefore, that Kerman designs
predominated. Other designs were borrowed
and still today there is no distinctive
Hereke design. Although wool rugs were
made there, Hereke is better known for its
very fine silks.

HERIZ *Persian, Map: G4, Plates 25, 26*
These rugs are renowned for their rectilinear
designs, a feature that is unusual in Iran
where the traditional prefers the arabesques
and scrolls so typical of Persian manufactory
rugs. This feature has been explained by some
authorities who are at pains to assert that the
Heriz weavers are incapable of weaving
anything other than straight lines. However,

even a cursory examination of some of the masterpieces from the looms of Heriz will dispel any belief that their weaving capabilities are limited. The more likely explanation is that they prefer the rectilinear style which has proved eminently successful in foreign markets for over a hundred years.

Plate 26 illustrates a wool Heriz made towards the last quarter of the nineteenth century. Rugs of this unusual shape were made at that time for the wealthy Viennese market where they were known as 'Iris' rugs.

The most important villages in the Heriz complex are Bakshis, Gorevan, Sarab, Ahar, Bilverdi, Kurdkendi, Meshgin, Jamalabad and Mehriban. A number of rugs were sold under the names of the villages where they were made but the names 'Ahar', 'Bakshis' and 'Gorevan' have come to be used as quality descriptions for rugs from this area.

HEYBEH
See Hehbehlik.

HILA (HILE) *Caucasian*
Those authors who mention this rug make no reference to a Chila and vice versa. Their descriptions of a Hila and their illustrations force one to the conclusion that they are different names for the same kind of rug. See Baku.

HINDUSTANIEH *Anatolian*
This is not an Indian rug as the name would seem to indicate but according to Mumford[58] the name was applied to a fine-quality rug from Demirçi in Turkey.

HISPANO-MORESQUE

In the context of carpets this name refers to those first made in Spain during the Moorish era. Some of the so-called 'Hispano-Moresque' carpets were subsequently attributed to the looms of Turkey. However, Spain has a recorded history of rug making dating from the twelfth century.

'HOLBEIN' *Anatolian*
The name is applied to a geometric style of Turkish rug believed to have been made for a period extending from the fifteenth to the seventeenth century. The name was acquired from such paintings as *The Ambassadors* (1533) by Hans Holbein the younger, now in the National Gallery, London, and his portrait of Georg Gisze (1532) which hangs in the Staatliche Museen, Berlin. The type of carpet which is depicted in the former painting is known as the 'large-pattern Holbein' and is believed to have been produced in the Bergama district of western Anatolia. The weave pattern of some of those of the type depicted in the Gisze portrait, or the 'small-pattern Holbein', clearly indicates an Ushak origin.

There are also the so-called 'Spanish Holbeins'. These are rugs of a similar geometric pattern, but made on the famous looms of Alcaraz in Spain during the second half of the fifteenth century.

HOUDJA *Caucasian*
See Karabagh.

HURJIN
See Kharjin.

82

HUSAINABAD (HOSSEINABAD) *Persian*
See Hamadan.

HYDERABAD *Indian, Map: O10*
Fine rugs were once made in the Pakistani (formerly Indian) town of that name, but the products of this century have been poor.

IBRAHIMABAD *Persian*
Town between Sultanabad and Qum which Albrecht Hopf says produced 'interesting individual pieces'.[59]

IDYAWAN (IDJEVAN) *Caucasian*
Kazak town and design name.

IGDYR *Turkoman*
It is believed that this tribe wove knotted carpets and it is quite likely that some surviving examples of their work are now commonly included in the broad designation of Yomut. It is not yet known what structural or design features, if any, are exclusive to the Igdyr rugs. Bogolyubov's Plate 16 is described as Igdyr.[60] See Yomut.

IKAT
Elaborate process in which the warp threads, cotton or silk, are tie-dyed in several colours before being attached to the loom. See Uzbek.

IMAMZADEH *Persian*
See Hamadan.

INCESU *Anatolian*
See Kayseri.

INDO-ISFAHAN *Indian*

Name applied to seventeenth and eighteenth-century Indian rugs which copied the classical Isfahan designs. The weave pattern of some of the Indo-Isfahans clearly shows that Isfahan weavers were responsible for their manufacture. See Mughal.

INELY (IGNELI, ENILE) *Anatolian*
This name has been used for the best rugs from Maden, and also occasionally for nineteenth and twentieth-century Ushaks.

INJELAS (INJELA, INGELES) *Persian, Map: H6*
Important weaving village south of Hamadan. See Hamadan.

INNICE *Anatolian*
See Kayseri and Konya.

'IRAN' *Persian*
Name once used to describe a type of rug supposed to be distinctive in design and structure. The term is seldom used nowadays except in the adjectival form of 'Iranian' as a generic term of derivation.

IRANSHAH *Persian*
See Bharistan.

IRIS *Persian*
At one time the products of Heriz were known outside Persia as Iris rugs, presumably a corruption of Heriz.

ISFAHAN (ISPAHAN, ISPHAHAN) *Persian, Map: I7, Plates 27, 28*
Two periods of rug manufacture are covered by this name. The classical Isfahans were

made in the sixteenth and seventeenth centuries and are believed to have been the creation of the court of Shah Abbas (1587-1629). This great period came to an end at the close of the seventeenth century when Isfahan ceased to be a rug weaving centre of any importance until the revival of the craft in the 1920s.

At the time when Mumford and Hawley wrote, 1900 and 1913 respectively, no rugs were being made in Isfahan. Today it is an important centre of the modern craft. Isfahan weavers, such as Serafian, have achieved great acclaim in the past thirty years.

Some nineteenth-century rugs have been attributed to Isfahan but the weave will indicate another provenance such as Sarouk.

ISFAHAN-BAKHTIARI *Persian*
Rugs made around Isfahan with Bakhtiari designs.

ISLAMABAD *Pakistan*
Modern rugs with designs derived from those of Kerman. It is not surprising that their importation into Iran is forbidden.

ISPARTA (SPARTA) *Anatolian, Map: B4*
This town, south-west of Konya, is a centre of modern commercial rug production. The products are sometimes sold as Smyrna rugs but more frequently as Isparta or Sparta. It is also an important market for the surrounding region, including the villages of Burdur, Çal, Zeyve, Denizli and Afyon, which produce largely Isparta-type rugs, often sold as such.

JABRAEEL *Caucasian*

See Karabagh.

JAHIZI
Dowry rugs received more care and attention in the making than other pieces, a fact that is exemplified by the Jahizi, Belouch dowry pieces.

JAHFER TABRIZ (JAHVER) *Persian*
See Tabriz.

JAMALABAD *Persian*
See Heriz.

JANGAL ARIQ *Afghanistan*
See Afghan.

JECHANEH *Persian*
See Hamadan.

JINJIN
See Djidjim.

JOI-NAMAZ (JA-I-NIMAZ) *Persian*
Mohammed enjoined that his followers should pray five times a day and observe cleanliness at all times. The corollary was that they should ensure that the place where they prayed was clean. There was no way of knowing whether or not the ground was unclean, in the desecrated sense of the word, so the custom grew of praying on a mat, or 'ja-i-nimaz' meaning 'the place of praying'. This is the correct Persian word for a prayer rug, though the rug trade also uses 'namazlik' and 'hatchli'. It appears that the term 'joi-namaz' is also used by the Turkoman.

JOLLAR *Turkoman*

Wide, shallow bag.

JORAGHAN *Persian*
See Hamadan.

JOSHAGAN (DJOUSHAGAN,
JOSHAGHAN, JUSHAQAN *Persian, Map: I6*
This village north of Isfahan has produced
rugs of renown for several centuries in a
characteristic design that still persists today.
Although these rugs came from the greater
Hamadan area, they formed a separate class
on the criterion of weave pattern.

Modern Joshagans are also produced in the
nearby village of Mei Mei. These are called
Mei Mei Joshagans but that name is
increasingly being used for the best quality
modern Joshagans, and does not necessarily
mean that the rugs so named were made in
Mei Mei village.

JOWAN TABRIZ *Persian*
See Tabriz.

JOZAN (JOSAN) *Persian*
Hamadan rug from the village of that name.
The name is also found in combination
with the word 'Sarouk' – as 'Jozan Sarouk'
– and this denotes the best quality rug
from Jozan.

JOZANDI QUM *Persian*
See Qum.

JUVAL (CHOUVAL, CHUVAL, JOUWAL)
The Turkish word for a bag is 'çuval'. The
word 'juval' and its variants is used for bags
or bag faces which measure roughly 100 cm
by 200 cm (3 ft 3 in. by 6 ft 6 in.) It is found

most commonly in association with the
products of the Turkoman tribes.

KABA-KARAMAN *Anatolian*
See Karaman.

KABISTAN (CABISTAN, COBISTAN,
GABYSTAN) *Caucasian*
Although one finds this name used less and
less frequently in the trade, some dealers
retain it with a personal confidence in its
meaning. This confidence is difficult to accept
as there is very little consensus of opinion as
to what the name includes or excludes in its
description. An attempt to define the
geographical limits of the name would
incorporate, albeit rather vaguely, the
Shirvan district and the southern part of the
Kuba district.

Various authorities have contrived to find a
derivation of the name. Some suggest that it
is a corruption of an incorrect name,
'Kubastan'. There is a town called Kuba but
Kubastan has never existed. Jacoby
considers that the term 'may be a contraction
of the words Kiaba-Shirvan, since Kiaba is
the designation of carpets . . . from 4'7" to
5'4" wide and 9'2" to 10' long'.[61] None of these
authors seem to be aware of the village of
Kobistan south-west of Baku and of the
district of the same name which stretches
from the Caspian Sea to west of Baku. It may
well be that originally the name Kabistan was
used to denote rugs that came from that area,
but by usage it has been extended to mean
different things to those of differing
experience. Even if one criticizes the most
modern classification of Caucasian rugs,

there is still no merit in perpetuating the use of the name Kabistan. It has no meaning on a structural basis and because of varying and vague usage as a designation of design or provenance it is also unacceptable either as a design or geographic classification.

KABUTARAHANG (KAPUTARAHANG)
Persian, Map: H6
The National Geographic Society used to spell the name as above, but more recently it has adopted the spelling 'Kabud Rahang'. The rugs made in this village fall into the Hamadan class.

KAFERO *Persian*
See Bakhtiari.

KAGISMAN *Anatolian*
Eastern Anatolian village and rug name.

KAIN *Persian*
See Qa'in.

KALAJUK *Persian*
See Hamadan.

KALARDASHT *Persian*
The name appeared in the twentieth century and is used to describe rugs made by the Lurs tribe in the Kellardasht area. See Lurs.

KALDARI *Afghanistan*
See Afghan.

KALI *Persian*
See Khali.

KALICHEH *Persian*

See Khali.

KALYK (CHALYK, KHALYK) *Turkoman*
Heavily fringed ornamental piece used in the wedding procession as part of the decoration on the bridal camel.

KANDAHAR (QANDAHAR) *Indian*
Although the city of this name is in south-eastern Afghanistan, the rugs so named are in fact made in India, not Afghanistan.

K'ANG *Chinese*
Form of furniture which the Chinese have used for a very long time and still use. It is a platform built at one end of the room and it is here that they sleep at night and sit during the day. On the side of the platform that faces into the room is a stove which heats the k'ang by a system of pipes. Rugs were spread on the k'ang and it appears that many Chinese as well as East Turkestan rugs were made for this purpose. These rugs were sometimes called 'Kong rugs' in the West.

KANGAL *Anatolian*
See Malatya.

KANSU *Chinese*
Rugs from two very different places are known by this name. The real Kansu rugs are made in Kansu and Suiyuan in China, while other rugs from East Turkestan which are sent to Peking are often sold there under this name by the Chinese merchants. Kansu is best known for saddle rugs. Suiyuan rugs, often sold as Kansu, are very similar to those of Kansu itself. See Paotou.

KAP *Turkoman*
Bag smaller than a torba; also called a 'mafresh'.

KAPUNNUK *Turkoman*
Knotted piece used as a decoration to frame the doorway of a tent (yurt).

KARABAGH *Caucasian, Map: G4/H4*
Plates 29, 30
These rugs were made in this region of the south-eastern Caucasus, bordering on north-eastern Iran. The products of this area have one of the few distinctive Caucasian weaves, a reliable feature of which is the double weft which occurs between every two rows of knots. Schürmann[62] subdivides this group on the basis of design into Chelaberd, Chondzoresk, Chan-Karabagh, Kasim-Ushag, Goradis, Shusha and Lampe-Karabagh. As pointed out under the entry 'Chondzoresk', this design is found both with the Karabagh and the Kazak weave. The design of the rug in Plate 30 is known as Chelaberd.

According to Dilley,[63] rugs from Karabagh were once sold under the names 'Houdja' and 'Jabraeel'.

KARACHOPH (KARACHOV, KARACHOP)
Caucasian, Map, see Karatchoph: G3
See Kazak.

KARADAGH *Persian, Map, see Qara Dagh Mountains: G4*
See Karaje.

KARAGASHLI *Caucasian, Map: H3*
Design subdivision of rugs from the Kuba area. See Daghestan and Kuba.

KARA GEUZ (KARAGÖS) *Persian*
District north-east of Hamadan where rugs of the Hamadan type are produced. A few authorities attribute a separate and distinctive rug to the Karaghuzlu tribe who inhabit the area.

KARAHISAR *Anatolian*
See Afyon.

KARAJA (KARADJA) *Persian*
The Qara Dagh – black mountains – are situated in north-western Iran bordering on the U.S.S.R. Just south of these mountains in the Qara Dagh region is the village of Karaja, north-west of Heriz. From the environs of this village comes a double-wefted knotted fabric of distinctive design known as a Karaja. Structurally these rugs are different from both the Heriz and Tabriz rugs. Edwards[64] referred to a single-wefted rug which he called Karaja but whether or not his reference was an error is not known. Single-wefted rugs are also produced in this area but they are not what we today call Karaja.

KARAJE *Persian*
Some authorities have used the names 'Karadagh' and 'Karaje' to describe tribal rugs from north-western Iran that differ from the more commercially orientated Karajas. Those that use both names attempt to differentiate between them but an analysis of the points of difference do not support a distinction. Other authorities maintain that 'Karaja' and 'Karaje' are alternate spellings for

the same name; yet others define a separate Kurdish weave from this area which they call a Karaje; and a few, either in desperation or discretion, ignore the names Karaja, Karaje and Karadagh altogether. But there is no doubt that single-wefted rugs with strong Caucasian design influences do come from the Qara Dagh region. Calling them Karaje may cause confusion with the Karajas; calling them all Kurdish may be ethnically incorrect and therefore Karadagh as a name of regional origin is to be preferred. See Ahmedabad.

KARAK (KHARAK) *Persian*
Donkey blanket.

KARAKEÇILI (KARAKECHI) *Anatolian*
Tribe living east of Balikesir whose small production is more usually sold under the name 'Balikesir'.

KARAKLIS *Caucasian*
Name of a town between Tiflis and Yerevan; also used to describe a particular type of Kazak rug.

KARAKALPAK *Turkoman, Map: L3*
This tribe lived in several groups in the region of the rivers Amu Darya and Syr Darya in Central Asia. Illustrations of some of the rare survivors of their knotted rugs are contained in books by Bogolyubov[65] and Schürmann.[66]

KARAMAN *Anatolian, Map: C4*
Also known as Kaba-Karaman. In the rug markets of Turkey all kelims were known as 'Karamani', meaning 'from Karaman', a province renowned for its kelims. All parts of

Turkey, however, produced and still produce kelims. A few knotted rugs of little consequence also come from this area.

KARA OSMAN GHIORDES *Anatolian*
Also known as Karaosmanoglu, meaning 'Kara, son of Osman'. As a rug name it is applied to Ghiordes rugs with a diaper pattern – which some refer to as a Kis Ghiordes pattern – and striking minor design features, the combination of which is exclusive to these rugs.

The only available reference to the derivation of the rug name is found in *Rugs in their Native Land*: 'At Magnesia, not far from Smyrna, lived and ruled the great feudal chief Kara Osman Oghlu. The splendour of his palace and his luxurious life reads like a tale from the Arabian Nights. He was a defier of Sultans and a regal lord. He commanded the Ghiordes weavers to make a special sort of rug for his exclusive use, and these carpets when they are to be found are called the Kara Osman Ghiordes.'[67] Unfortunately the author does not quote her authority for this story, nor does she say when the great feudal chief lived.

KARAPINAR *Anatolian*
Rugs of this name come from the village of Karapinar near Konya. They are usually classified in the Konya group but would more correctly be referred to as a separate and individual group.

KARKIN *Afghanistan*
See Afghan.

KARS *Anatolian, Map: F3*

This town in eastern Anatolia, near the border of Soviet Armenia, is surrounded by peoples of various ethnic groups: Tartars, Armenians, Georgians, Azerbaijanis, Circassians, Turkomans, Kurds and Yürüks. Many of the rugs produced by these groups are sold under the name of Kars, and include the so-called 'Turkish Kazaks' of the last century as well as more recent work. These are distinguishable from the true Kazaks by their weave and colour, but show marked Kazak design influence. They could have been made by almost any of the ethnic groups in the area. Rugs have been made in eastern Anatolia for a very long time and it is possible that some of the 'dragon carpets' of the sixteenth and seventeenth centuries came from there.

KASHAN (KESHAN) *Persian, Map: 16, Plates 31, 32*
Town in central Iran between Isfahan and Tehran that has been renowned for its rugs for centuries. Similar to many other important rug-making centres, the production in Kashan virtually ceased after the Afghan invasion in the early eighteenth century. The late nineteenth century saw a revival of the craft and the modern rugs of Kashan are once more among the best made in Iran.

The revival of the rug craft in Kashan at the end of the nineteenth century has been attributed by Edwards[68] to the enterprise of Hajji Mollah Hassan who procured the weaving of rugs with a surplus of Australian merino wool purchased from Manchester. Edwards may well be correct but local lore attributes the revival to Zufilkhar Ed Din

Mochtashem, governor of Kashan. The rugs of this era made in merino wool are frequently referred to as Motashem, or its alternative forms – Monchtashemi, Mochtashan or Mochtashem. They were made for about thirty years from the end of the nineteenth century.

The 'Manchester Kashans' are not, as the name would seem to imply, Kashan-designed rugs made in Manchester; neither are they rugs made with merino wool that came from Manchester, nor were the ones we have seen made in Kashan, but in the Sultanabad area. This unhappy name only appears in the U.S.A. market and although its derivation is obscure, a suggestion is made under the entry 'Mahadjiran'.

The word 'kurk' which signifies the winter clip from the sheep's neck, the best clip of all, is also occasionally used to describe the best quality wool rugs from Kashan, made since the revival. See Harun and Aliabad.

KASHGAR *Chinese Turkestan, Map: Q4*
Rugs of this name are very difficult to distinguish from those that are called 'Khotans' and 'Yarkands' and which also come from Chinese Turkestan. Kashgar, Khotan and Yarkand are names of important towns where rugs were made and also where those from the surrounding areas were marketed. The distinction between the rugs of these different names is based solely on design and colour.

KASHKAI *Persian*
See Qashqa'i.

KASHMAR *Persian*

See Khorasan and Turshiz.

KASHMIR *Map: R6*
This name was once used in Europe for soumaks from the Caucasus. There is a type of modern Indian rug called a Kashmir.

KASIM-USHAG *Caucasian*
Design subdivision of Karabagh rugs.

KASVIN (GASVIN, KAZVIN, QASVIN) *Persian, Map: H5*
For a short period the capital of the early Safavid Shahs. Tahmasp (1524-1587) moved the capital from Tabriz to Kasvin because Tabriz was very vulnerable to Turkish attack, and was in fact invaded by the Ottomans three times in the sixteenth century. Tahmasp's successor, Shah Abbas (1587-1629) moved his capital to Isfahan in 1590.

Some early authorities believed that certain rugs now attributed to Isfahan were made in Kasvin. There is no evidence for this, apart from a reasonable assumption that a court manufactory existed there at the time when it was the Safavid capital.

Kasvin is also a misleading trade name for a type of modern Hamadan.

KATCHLI (KATCHOI)
Alternative spellings of 'hatchli'.

KAVAK *Anatolian*
See Malatya.

KAYSERI *Anatolian, Map: D4*
Capital of the Kayseri province and major rug market of central Turkey. Modern rugs are produced and sold under this name including silks that rival the modern Herekes. A rug sold at Kayseri could come from any one of a number of central Anatolian villages and their surrounding farms, among them the villages of Bunyan, Innice, Kovak, Obruk (often also sold as Konya Obruk), Selçuk, Incesu, Avanos, and Urgüp. A number of these are sometimes used as rug names.

Rugs have apparently been made in Kayseri for many centuries as Marco Polo referred to those he had seen on his travels there in 1271. See Panderma.

KAZAK (KAZAKH) *Caucasian, Map, see Kazakh: G3, Plates 33, 34*
At the beginning of the twentieth century, the names Tcherkess, Kutais, Tiflis, Georgian, Armenian and Kazak were applied to the various Caucasian weaves found in the region west of Karabagh and south of the Greater Caucasus. Nowadays all but the name Kazak have largely disappeared except among the doyens of the trade who rightly assert that neither does the modern classification of the Kazaks comprise a group that is homogeneous on a basis of design or structure, nor is it likely that they were all made by the same tribe or group.

Schürmann[69] has subdivided the Kazak group into Bordjalou, Idyawan, Karachoph, Karaklis, Fachralo, Lombalo, Lori-Pombak, Schulaver, Sewan and Shikli. Most of these are names of towns and villages but it is doubtful if all the rugs bearing a particular design were made in the village after which the design is now widely known, thanks largely to Schürmann. Even if not altogether valid as a classification by provenance, these names provide a convenient nomenclature for designs.

In discussing structure, Schürmann[70] says that one of the distinguishing features of the Kazak class is that both warps to which a knot is tied lie on an even plane. This, however, cannot be considered a constant feature because in some of his subdivisions a depressed warp is a common occurrence. Structurally the Kazaks do display a number of common features: they are knotted with the symmetrical (Turkish) knot; the warp and weft are almost always wool, the former generally undyed and the latter dyed; and the pile is wool; on the line of the warp threads the knots are longer than they are wide; and the weft crosses two or more times between each row of knots without apparent order.

The confusion that surrounds Kazak rugs is largely due to the strange phenomenon of the existence of the name in south-western Caucasia. The word 'khazaki' itself is problematical as there are two distinct groups of people who bear the name, and neither of them seems to have anything to do with knotted rugs nor with the southern Caucasus. The word means 'adventurer', 'freebooter' or 'rider of the steppes' in the Turkic languages and it was adopted into Russian at the time of the Tartar invasions. It is only fair to say that not everyone agrees even with that statement and some suggest that the Russian word had a quite separate origin. To those who have no emotional involvement in the issue that seems unlikely in view of the evidence.

The word 'khazaki' is perhaps best known as applying to the Russian Cossacks who were Christians. It also applies to a group of Muslim Turkic people living in what became known as Khazakstan in Central Asia. There is no ethnic connection between the two groups, though the word was already in use in the fifteenth century to describe both groups.

How then did the name reach the southern Caucasus? And how did it come to apply to so large and varied a group of rugs? It has been variously suggested that the name Kazakh, as it occurs in the Caucasian town and district, derives from firstly, the Russian word for the Cossacks, 'Khazaki'; secondly, that it is the same root word as Circassian; and thirdly, that it came from the Central Asian Khazak tribe.

The town of Kazakh is in the Kwemo Kartli district which is bounded by the Mtkvari, Debeda and Akstafa Rivers. The surrounding district was, until taken over by the Kingdom of Georgia, ruled by the Princes of Kazak and Karketli, about whom little is known.

On the evidence which is too lengthy to set out here, it is unlikely that the Cossacks are responsible for the name as firstly, they are not known ever to have made knotted rugs, and secondly, they never formed settlements south of the Greater Caucasus. The Cossack line which was established by Russia to protect its boundary against the incursions of the Caucasian tribes was north of the Caucasus. Another group of Cossacks was settled for some time to the east, in northern Daghestan on the Terek River, but this was a long way from the town of Kazakh. Cossacks were sent by the Tsar in 1556 to protect King Levan of Karketli from Turkish attack, but this group was soon withdrawn when Persia objected to its presence. In any case they were considerably to the west of the region under discussion.

The suggestion that links the word 'Circassian' with Kazak was made by George Vernadsky, who says that 'the word derives from the ethnic name, Kas, an old north Caucasian people now known as Adyge or Circassians. The latter name in the original form of Chahar-Kas, means four Kas clans. In Russian since the fifteenth century the name has been used in the form Cherkasy. The name appears in the Codex Cumanicus in the form Cosac (written around 1294). In the Synaxarion of Sugdaia of the twelfth century there is a supplementary entry dated May 17th, 1308, concerning a young Christian killed by the sword of the Kazaks. In my opinion, here again the Kasogi (Circassians) are meant.'[71] For several reasons this explanation is not convincing as the origin of the Caucasian Kazakh, particularly as the Circassians were north-west Caucasians and quite different people from those living in the southern area which we are discussing.

Mumford described the weavers of the Kazak rugs as a 'tribe of nomad Kazaks inhabiting the hills about Nova Bayesid and Lake Gotcha in Erivan. They are an offshoot of the great hordes whose home is in the Khirghiz steppes and whose kinsmen are scattered over the southern districts of Russia away to the banks of the Don.'[72] Mumford probably came closer to the truth than any other commentator. We know that the migration of Seljuk Turks from Central Asia set off a surge into Armenia and Anatolia via Persia as early as the tenth century, a movement that continued in waves for many centuries and explains the Turkicization of the southern Caucasus and may also explain the existence of the knotting craft in that area.

Whoever the founders of the town and district of Kazakh were, the inhabitants of the area have for some time been a mixture of people including Armenians – who are Christian – and Turkic and Kurdish tribes – who are Muslim. All these people appear to have been producers of knotted rugs. It is often said that Kazak rugs woven by Armenians can sometimes be recognized by the symbol of the Christian cross in their rug designs. We cannot say if this is a valid association; nor, indeed, can we point to any structural features which are peculiar to these Armenian rugs.

KEEN-LUND (CH'IEN LUNG)
Trade name for a type of modern Indian rug with a Chinese design. Ch'ien Lung is the Chinese name from which it is obviously derived. See Chinese.

KELARDASHT *Persian*
See Kalardasht and Lurs.

KELIM (KHILIM, KILIM, GILLIM, GHILIM, CHELIM)
The word is best used to describe tapestry-woven rugs. Oriental kelims are most often weft-faced, meaning that the weft threads hide the warp, and provide the colour and pattern of the rugs. The weaving of kelims is thought to be a very ancient craft but as they are not as resistant to wear as knotted work, none that are believed to be older than the seventeenth century have survived. Kelims are made in all parts of the Oriental rug-weaving world.

KELLEGI (KELLEY, KELLAI) *Persian*
Head carpet of a set. The term is used to describe rugs of a certain size, 152 cm to 183 cm by 305 cm to 366 cm (5ft to 6ft by 10ft to 12ft). See Kenareh.

KENAREH (KENARE)
The Persian composition of floor rugs in the main assembly room was a large central carpet called the 'mian farsh' flanked on either side by the long narrow 'kenarehs'. A fourth and smaller carpet, laid across the top of the arrangement at the head of the room, was the 'kellegi'.

'Kenareh' in Persian means 'sea shore', and is the term used in the trade to describe runners roughly 1m wide (3ft 4 in. or 1 'zar') with the length varying between 488 cm (16ft) and 762 cm (25ft).

KENDIRLI *Anatolian*
Name applied most commonly to Kula rugs that were made with an intermittent weft of dimension thicker than the rest of the weft shoots. See Kula.

KENGUERLU *Caucasian*
Trade name once used for Caucasian rugs. The name embraced rugs from various areas and has been supplanted by a variety of descriptions.

KERDAR *Persian*
See Hamadan.

KERKI *Turkoman, Map: M5*
Central Asian town on the Amu Darya near the present-day boundary between Turkmenistan and Afghanistan. Applied to rugs, the name is a colour subclassification of Ersari work produced in the Kerki area and marketed there.

KERMAN (KIRMAN) *Persian, Map: J8, Plates 35, 36*
The locality of this area is remote and its unattractive, harsh natural features are no magnet to friend or foe. The poorest province of Iran has nevertheless produced weavers of renown since at least the late sixteenth century when Shah Abbas established one of a number of royal manufactories in the city of Kerman. The fact that the city was chosen as a site for a royal manufactory, a long way from the court, indicates that here there was already a tradition of excellent weaving.

Unfortunately there are no surviving examples of Kerman work that pre-date the late sixteenth century or early seventeenth century. From literary sources we know that Yezd, to the north-west of Kerman, at one time produced carpets equal, if not superior, to those of Kerman. No carpets of this early period have been positively attributed to Yezd and therefore one cannot comment on any distinguishing features that may have existed between the products of the two cities; but by a process of elimination it may yet be possible to do so. We refer in this regard to the carpets made in the 'vase technique', a phrase invented by Dr May H. Beattie to describe carpets of a like technique, some of which were exhibited in Sheffield and Birmingham from April to July 1976, under the title 'Carpets of Central Persia'. We believe that this was the first exhibition of carpets chosen because of their structural similarity and it therefore represents a giant step forward in the methodology of Oriental rug studies. With the greatest respect to Dr Beattie, and possibly with some temerity, we suggest that these carpets can be attributed to two manufactories, if not to two centres, of which Kerman was one.

It is interesting to note that the dyers of Kerman are renowned for their skill in producing light shades of colour. This traditional skill appears to be centuries old.

To the north of Kerman is the village of Ravar which has a rug weaving history at least as long as that of Kerman. The name, usually corrupted to 'Laver', has been lent to the rugs called 'Kerman Lavers' or 'Ravars' which have acquired a renown greater than Kermans. There are possibly two reasons for this. In the first place they are rarer than Kermans and secondly, the name is frequently used as a quality description though authorities disagree as to whether a 'Laver' is coarser or finer than a Kerman.

During the 1930s Kermans in a particular design and colour, neither truly traditional, were produced for the U.S.A. market. This gave rise to the term 'Eski Kerman' invented among the Istanbul dealers and meaning 'Old Kermans'. 'Eski Kerman' referred to the old Kermans as well as the newer but still traditional ones, and distinguished them from the product made for foreigners. See Zhupar.

KERMANSHAH *Persian, Map: G6*
This town was on the ancient route of the caravans travelling from the East to Baghdad and Antioch. Its locality made it an important bazaar town where the rugs of the surrounding Kurdish and Luri nomads were sold. Although these rugs were made by different people in different designs and techniques, they nevertheless acquired the name of the town where they were bought, an incident of common occurrence in the rug world.

Whether the designs which are attributed to Kermanshah originated in manufactories, which no doubt operated there in the days of its importance, and the designs were subsequently perpetuated by the nomads, or whether the manufactories borrowed from the nomads, are questions that are unanswerable.

The Kermanshah rugs of this century are made in manufactories elsewhere in Iran. The name now denotes a design but not the provenance of these pieces.

KESHKULI *Persian*
See Qashqa'i.

KEŞIMUSLU *Anatolian*
See Konya.

KHALABAR *Indian*
Type of manufactory rug which appeared in the twentieth century.

KHALI (KALI, GHALI, CHALI, QALI)
Persian and Turkish word for a carpet. Kalicheh (Khalidje, Galidshe) is the diminutive form. The Turkoman equivalents are often written as 'Qalin' and 'Qalincha'.

KHALYK (CHALYK, KALYK) *Turkoman*
See Kalyk.

KHAMSEH *Persian, Map, see Khamseh*

94

Confederation: I8/J8
This name refers to two distinct weaving areas. The Khamseh district in north-western Iran produces rather inferior rugs woven in the Hamadan technique. In south-western Iran, east of Shiraz, is the Khamseh Confederation which is composed of five different tribes or subgroups, namely, Arab, Basiri, Ainalu, Baharlu and Nafar. The rugs produced in the Confederation are all single-wefted. The Arab, Basiri and Nafar use the symmetrical knot whereas the Baharlu use both the symmetrical and asymmetrical knots.

The older weavings of the Baharlu were highly regarded but today the Confederation rarely produces anything of better than bazaar quality.

KHARAK
See Karak.

KHARJIN (CHOURDJIN, KHOURDJIN, KURJIN, HURJIN)
Saddle bag with two pockets usually measuring about 122 cm by 61 cm (4ft by 2ft). O'Bannon says the word literally means 'donkey pocket'.[73]

KHEYB *Caucasian*
Type of large bag.

KHILIM
See Kelim.

KHIVA *Turkestan, Map: L3*
There is no evidence that any rugs were produced in this town or Khanate that can correctly be called 'Khiva' in preference to the more appropriate name of the tribe that made them. Earlier this century the better quality Ersari Afghan rugs were often known in the trade as 'Khiva rugs'. See Ersari.

KHOI *Persian*
See Tabriz.

KHOJA (CHOJA, HOJA)
See Yomut.

KHORASAN (KHURASAN, KHORASSAN)
Persian, Map: K5/K6/L5/L6, Plates 37, 38
Meaning 'the land of the rising sun', Khorasan is the largest of Iran's provinces. In earlier times when borders were either non-existent or at least of very little significance, the name was understood to embrace a much larger area than the present province and it then included Merv and Herat.

From the area that is now the Khorasan province came the rugs of the Baluchi, the Iranian Turkoman and those described as Meshed and Khorasan. The latter two are really arbitrary divisions of the same group as it became customary to identify as 'Meshed' a finer-woven, shorter-clipped Khorasan. Those two features can never be the sole indices of provenance, however, as the premises preclude normal variations of craftsmanship that are found in every group. The idea of calling the finer woven rugs 'Meshed', probably arose out of a natural inclination to associate the best rugs with the holy city which is in Khorasan, and which, to the Shi'ite Muslim, ranks third in sanctity after Mecca and Medina.

The weave of Khorasan rugs is patently

different from any others, a fact which, coupled with a common use of a blue weft, makes them one of the easiest Persian rug types to identify. See Plate 37.

In alphabetical order, the most important rug names of the Khorasan group are Asghand, Birjand, Dorosch, Kashmar (previously called Turshiz), Meshed, Mud, Qa'in and Sabsawar. These were all weaving centres but some of the names are also used as quality descriptions, regrettably without much consistency. For example, the Birjands have been variously described as the best and the worst of the Khorasans. The reason lies in the fact that over the decades not everyone has had the same experience of the rugs from this area. The Birjands were formerly very good, but have declined to the extent that today they are aptly described as inferior Khorasans. See Farsibaff, Tiebaff and Turkibaff.

KHOREY *Persian*
See Bakhtiari.

KHOTAN *East Turkestan, Map: R5, Plates 39, 40*
Name used for rugs from east Central Asia which were produced in the town of that name and in the surrounding area. These rugs were formerly known as Samarkand, which was the major city of Central Asia and therefore an important market. Unfortunately their wool pile is soft and not durable and the weave is generally loose, a combination which results in rather few extant pieces. Khotan was on the Silk Road as was Samarkand and many silk as well as wool rugs were made there. Structurally these rugs

cannot be distinguished from Kashgars. With difficulty, though with some validity, a distinction can be made on a colour and design basis.

KHOURDJIN
See Kharjin.

KIBITKA
Russian word commonly used in place of the Turkoman 'ev' or 'yurt' and the Kirghiz 'aladjak' to describe a tent. Kibitka is also used for the functional and decorative bands which were hung round the interior of the tent. Used in this sense, it is found alone or as 'kibitka strips' an alternate term being 'Bokhara strips'. These 'tent bands', as they are most commonly called now, are made either in kelim work, or entirely knotted, or in a combination of both. Other names for tent bands are 'bou', 'yolami' and 'yup'.

KILIM
See Kelim.

KIRGHIZ *Central Asia, Map: O3*
Non-Turkoman people of the Central Asian steppes who wove rugs that have generally been described as inferior copies of various Turkoman designs. Unfortunately too few appear for positive identification or more constructive comment. Grote-Hasenbalg,[74] Schürmann,[75] and Bogolyubov[76] provide illustrations of Kirghiz rugs in their books.

KIRMAN *Persian, Map, see Kerman: J8*
See Kerman.

KIRNE *Anatolian*

This name might occasionally be used for the soumaks and kelims made in the village of Kirne.

KIRSHEHIR (KIRŞEHIR) *Anatolian, Map, see Kirşehir: C3, Plates 41, 42*
Capital of the Turkish province of the same name. Although carpet weaving is a major activity in the area, Kirshehirs are mainly known as prayer rugs. The design of these rugs is very similar to the Mudjurs but as far as the nineteenth-century rugs are concerned they can be distinguished from each other by their weave patterns. Design subdivisions are the Kirshehir-Medjidi and Kirshehir-Sinekli.

KIZIL AYAK (KIZYL-AYAK, QIZILAYAK) *Turkoman, Map, see Kizyl Ayak: M5/N5 Plates 43, 44*
Barthold[77] refers to Abul-Ghazi, who was Khan of Khiva in the middle of the seventeenth century, spending the winter among the Kizil Ayak division of the Ersari tribe near Meihane. This reference probably accounts for a number of people considering the Kizil Ayak as an offshoot of the Ersari. Wegner,[78] on the other hand, maintains that they cannot be regarded as of the Ersari group. Even if they were at one time an offshoot of the Ersari, by the eighteenth and nineteenth centuries they appear to have become very independent of the Ersari if their weavings are anything to go by. Neither design nor weave pattern remotely resembles Ersari work.

Whatever the ethnic origin of these people may be, the problem is in no way simplified by the weavings attributed to them. The magnificent door-hanging illustrated as a Saryk (Plate 68) would generally be called a Kizil Ayak in the rug trade. Some authorities draw a distinction between those with the colouring of this rug, and others of like design but lighter in colour – such as Bogolyubov's Plate 4.[79] The latter type are usually attributed to the Saryk. We believe that both types were made by the Saryk but from different areas and we base our opinion on the weave pattern. The colour difference suggests that different areas are involved.

The carpet illustrated in Plate 44 was made by the Kizil Ayak. We are not alone in this assertion which is made with as much confidence as is possible in the realms of a folkcraft where the verbal evidence is no longer available to support conclusions drawn from surviving artefacts. We have found the weave pattern of this carpet in all carpets and juvals attributed with the same confidence to the Kizil Ayak. We have also found this weave pattern in some of the door-hangings attributed to the Kizil Ayak, but the weave pattern illustrated in Plate 67 is not one of them. The weave pattern of that particular piece is that of the Saryk and our conclusion is therefore inescapable. See Afghan and Saryk.

KOKAND (KOKUND) *East Turkestan, Map: O4*
This city in the Fergana Valley dates from at least the tenth century when it was known as Kavakend. It was an important trading centre and at one time lent its name to rugs marketed there. There is, however, no distinct Kokand rug though the area does have a long tradition of textile manufacture.

97

KOLIAYEH *Persian*
Type of rug from Iranian Kurdistan that
structurally would fall within the Hamadan
group.

KOLTUK (GALTUK, GOLTUK, KULTUK)
Persian
Only three authors mention rugs of this
name. Mumford[80] and Jacoby[81] indicate a
Kurdish provenance, whereas Hubel[82]
assigns them to the Hamadan class. The name
is no longer acknowledged and even when it
was, Mumford said that the rugs could not be
given the benefit of a class. They were
probably a design classification of rugs from
north-western Persia, possibly of Kurdish
origin.

KOLVANAQ *Persian*
Twentieth-century rug of the Heriz type from
the village of the same name.

KOMARLU KULA (KEMARJU, KOMARJU,
KOMURJU) *Anatolian*
See Kula.

KONAGHEND (KONAKHKEND) *Caucasian,
Map: H3*
See Kuba.

KONAKCHA
See Tainaksha.

KONG RUGS *Chinese*
See K'ang.

KONYA (KONIA, KONIEH) *Anatolian,
Map: C4*

The accepted spelling of the name of this
town is 'Konya'. It is one of the oldest
continuously occupied urban centres in the
world. The Seljuk sultans of Rum made it
their capital and it was they who changed its
name from the Greek name, Iconium, to
Konya.

The earliest mention of carpet weaving in
Konya dates from the report of Marco Polo's
travels there in the thirteenth century. At that
time there probably were carpet
manufactories attached to the Seljuk courts
and large carpets and fragments of that period
were found early this century in the Alâadin
Mosque in Konya. These are now in the
Museum of Turkish and Islamic Arts in
Istanbul.

Rugs are still woven in the surrounding
area and the products of the following
villages, among others – as well as of the rural
area – are usually sold as Konya: Davaç,
Keşimuslu, Karapinar, Obruk, and
Tashpinar. Many rugs, such as those from the
nearby villages of Kozak, Innice and Selçuk,
though of the Konya type, are according to
Iten-Maritz,[83] largely sold in Kayseri and
Nigde which are more active markets.

Although Ladik falls within the boundaries
of the Konya province or 'il', its rugs are
distinguishable from those of Konya. Within
the Konya class one can also distinguish
between the products of the villages and the
rural areas. The example shown in Plates 81
and 82 is a rural weave made as a bed or
'yatak'. Rugs of this design and shape are
sometimes ascribed to the Yürüks from the
Konya area. The weave pattern of these rugs
is different from that of the Yürüks of other
areas. See Yürük.

98

KOUHI AFSHAR *Persian*
See Afshar.

KOUM *Persian*
See Qum.

KOUMAT *Persian*
See Gumbat

KOVAK *Anatolian*
See Kayseri.

KOY (KHOY, KHOI, CHOY) *Persian*
See Tabriz.

KOZAK *Anatolian*
Village rug of the Konya district. See Konya.

KOZAN *Anatolian*
According to Mumford, rugs sold under this name are similar 'to Mosul Kurd fabrics in texture and quality'.[84] The village of Kozan is south-east of Nigde and if rugs are still produced there no other reference to them has been found – unless they are the same as Hawley's Gozene. See Gozene.

KUBA *Caucasian, Map: H3, Plates 11, 12, 71, 72*
Historically, the district of Daghestan is much older than this town which falls within its boundaries. It is, therefore, not surprising that there is confusion between rugs called 'Daghestan' and others called 'Kuba'. In fact, the differences in weave which can be seen in the Chi Chi (Plate 11), Seyshour (Plate 71), Chila (Plate 3) and Daghestan (Plate 13) are all to be found within each of the Shirvan, Kuba, Daghestan and Baku groups. The

classification of these groups cannot be justified on the basis of weaving technique but is largely one of convenience based on design differences.

The 'dragon carpets' were originally called Armenian. At least some of them are now attributed to the Kuba area. Both attributions may be completely accurate as some of them may well have been made by Armenians in the Kuba area.

Design subdivisions of the Kuba group are Alpan-Kuba, Karagashli, Konaghend, Chi Chi, Perepedil, Seyshour and Zejwa. See 'Dragon Kuba' and Daghestan.

KUDUANI *Persian*
See Belouch.

KULA (KULAH) *Anatolian, Map: B3, Plates 45, 46*
This town is a short distance south of Ghiordes, and it is, therefore, not surprising that there is a marked similarity between the rugs of these two areas. Although the designs of the typical examples from each area are readily recognized, not infrequently there are overlaps which even experts find impossible to identify positively as coming from one or the other place.

Structurally the Kulas have a very pronounced depression of the warp, sometimes to the extent that one warp is almost totally concealed by its partner, whereas the depression of the alternate warps in the Ghiordes is of a minor degree. It appears that the occasional use of a jute weft is a feature unique to some of the coarser Kula rugs.

The following names prefixed to Kula are

found in the rug trade: Komarlu (Kemarju, Komarju, Komurju), the 'charcoal carpets', so called because of their sombre colouring; Kafarli, a design description whose derivation is unknown; Mazerlik (Mazarlik), more commonly known in the West as 'graveyard Kulas'. According to some, this is an interpretation of the design with its pictures of cypresses and tombs. It seems that these rugs were used for funeral rites – the dead were carried to the cemetery in them – and as they were only used for this purpose, many have survived; Demirçi Kulas which are not Kulas at all, but were made in Demirçi, north of Ghiordes; Kendirli, as applied to Kulas, referring to a structural feature where wefts of an abnormal thickness – three and four ply – are used, but the name is very rarely heard among Western dealers.

KUM *Persian, Map, see Qum: I6*
See Qum.

KUM KAPU (KOUM KA-POUR) *Anatolian*
The filatures at Broussa and in its environs assured the Istanbul weavers of a plentiful supply of silk. This situation inspired the creation of the Hereke manufactory and, at the end of the last century, the manufactories of Kum Kapu and Top Kapu. The former name means 'gate of the sand', 'Kum' meaning 'sand' and 'Kapu' meaning 'gate', and originates from the gate of the fortress of Justinian which opens onto a beach of the Sea of Marmara.

It appears that the name Kum Kapu is being used by some as a quality description for the finest woven silk rugs from the Istanbul manufactories. There are two reasons for suggesting this. Firstly, the Kum Kapu manufactory operated between 1890 and 1910 and produced only a few rugs every year, but the number of rugs called 'Kum Kapu' in circulation indicates that far more are sold than were ever made. Secondly, like the other Istanbul manufactories the products of Kum Kapu were copies of antique designs, mostly Persian, rendered with varying degrees of success. The silk rugs of Hereke, Istanbul and Kum Kapu are all made in the same technique. It is true that a lot of Herekes bear the mark of the manufactory but there are many that do not. In the absence of that mark the attribution of a silk rug to Hereke, Kum Kapu or Istanbul would not be blessed with a consensus of expert opinion.

KUNDUZ
See Afghan.

KURBAN DAI *Persian*
See Tabriz and Kurdish.

KURDISH *Anatolian and Persian, Map: F4/ F5/G5/G6*
Larger Kurdistan includes that part of eastern Turkey where the eastern extension of the Tauros Mountains lies, northern Iraq, the southernmost parts of the Caucasus and Soviet Armenia, and north-western Iran. Rugs are produced in all of these areas and therefore a Kurdish rug should refer to a rug made somewhere within these boundaries. In the trade a Kurdish rug generally refers to one made in Iranian Kurdistan. This province or 'ostan' is bounded by Iraq in the west, Azerbaijan in the east and the ostan of Kermanshahan in the south. The area

includes the rugs of Bijar and Senneh but Kurdish rugs are as different from either of them as the rugs of Bijar and Senneh are from each other, although they are all products of Kurdish people. That there are those differences is not surprising considering the size of the area and the extent and variety of the influences at work. Even the way of life differs between the groups. The majority are settled agriculturalists but some are still semi-nomadic and practise transhumance – that is, the movement between summer pastures on the mountain slopes and winter quarters in the valleys and lowlands – despite the difficulties imposed by virtually closed borders.

It is a pity that the word 'Kurdish' has tended to become confined to north-western Iran because it has meant that Kurdish products outside of that area have had to find unsatisfactory and inaccurate labels, such as 'Turkish Kazaks' and 'Yürüks'; some of the rugs so called are undoubtedly Kurdish. The confusion even extends to the use of the name 'Kazak' to describe Kurdish rugs that bear some resemblance to the true Kazak. In those instances, although the design influence is apparent, the structure clearly indicates a Kurdish provenance. The name 'Kurd Kazak' for these rugs is a reasonable attempt at dealing with the problem, but it must also be realized that a Kurd Kazak could have come from eastern Anatolia or much of the south-western Caucasian country, as there have been groups of Kurds living throughout this region for probably much more than a hundred years.

Although there are tribal subdivisions of the Kurdish people, one rarely finds their names used as rug descriptions. An exception is the Qulyahi; this may be because their rug production was larger than the other tribes and therefore more widely known.

The Kurds are a mountain people, thought to be a blend of the invading Medes, an Aryan people like the Iranians, and the earlier inhabitants of what is now Kurdistan. They are an independent-minded people, very aware of their own identity, and proud of their history. The great Muslim leader, Saladin, famed for his successes as well as his chivalry in the crusades, was a Kurd.

KURD KAZAK *Anatolian*
See Turkish Kazak.

KURDKENDI *Persian*
Village rug of the Heriz area. See Heriz.

KURDLAR *Persian*
Modern rug of the Heriz type.

KURJIN *Turkoman*
See Kharjin.

KURK KASHAN *Persian*
See Kashan.

KUTAIS (KUTAISI) *Caucasian, Map, see Kutaisi: F3*
See Georgian.

KUTAHYA *Anatolian, Map: B3*
Rug weaving town in Turkey producing modern rugs which are more commonly sold under the names of Ghiordes or Ushak.

101

KUTLU *Persian*
See Afshar.

LABIJAR (LEBJAR)
See Afghan.

LADIK *Anatolian, Map: C4, Plates 47, 48*
Corruption of 'Laodicea', the name of two other Asia Minor cities. All three were named after Laodice the wife of Antiochus III (242-187 B.C.), the most successful of the Seleucid kings.

The rug weaving centre of Ladik is situated a short distance north-west of Konya. Although rug weaving appears to have commenced there probably only in the late seventeenth or the eighteenth century, it produced a style of its own and even influenced the rugs of Konya which has a much longer weaving history. One hears the name of Konya Ladik used to denote the products of Konya made with a Ladik design.

The earlier Ladiks were acclaimed as of the finest of Turkish weaves but the modern rugs are degenerate versions of the antiques. This is a valid generalization, which is regrettably applicable to almost all modern Turkish rugs. Plates 47 and 48 illustrate a rug of the late eighteenth or early nineteenth century.

LAHORE *Indian, Map: P7*
Second largest city of Pakistan, it enjoyed its golden age during the reign of the Mughals which began in 1524. Lahore occasionally was a place of royal residence at that time. With the aid of Persian weavers the Mughal emperors were responsible for the beginning of the rug manufactories in India, which of course included at that time the area which is now Pakistan. Although the Persian influence was strong, a distinctive Mughal style did nevertheless develop. The Mughal designs have long since vanished, though knotted rugs are still made in Lahore today. Many of these are poor quality copies of Persian designs, a favourite being the Abadeh. The name Lahore is also used to denote a lighter quality of Pak Bokhara. See Pak Bokhara.

LAMBALO (LOMBALO) *Caucasian, Map: G3, Plates 33, 34*
See Kazak.

LAMPE-KARABAGH *Caucasian*
See Karabagh.

LANBARAN *Persian*
Modern village rug from Azerbaijan in north-western Iran.

LARISTAN *Persian*
District in south-western Iran from which a certain number of tribal rugs used to come to Western markets. The production, at least for commercial purposes, seems to have ceased. The name was at one time used in the rug trade for the tribal and village rugs now known as Niriz (Neyriz). The town of Niriz is north of this area and probably was an important market place. Some dealers early in the twentieth century used the name Laristan and also Shahristan, Iranshah and Bharistan for certain rugs made in India and Bulgaria. Fortunately, this practice seems to have ceased though equally odd and confusing ones continue. See Niriz and Trade Names.

102

LAVER *Persian*
See Kerman.

LEBJAR
See Labijar.

LENKORAN *Caucasian, Map: H4*
See Talish.

LESGHI *Caucasian, Map, see Lesghistan: H2*
See Daghestan.

LILIHAN *Persian*
Modern type of rug from the Sultanabad (Arak) region which differs from the other Sultanabad fabrics in that it is single-wefted. Lilihan is one of a group of Armenian villages which makes the rugs known as Lilihan.

LOMBALO (LAMBALO) *Caucasian, Map, see Lambalo: G3, Plates 33, 34*
See Kazak.

LORI *Persian*
See Lurs.

LORI-POMBAK (LORI-PAMBAK) *Caucasian, Map: G3*
See Kazak.

'LOTTO' *Anatolian*
Although these carpets were depicted by a number of artists, they take their name from the paintings of Lorenzo Lotto (1480-1556) such as the altar-piece in the Zanipolo Church, Venice, and his painting of a family group in the National Gallery, London.

The weave of the surviving rugs of this type confirms the consensus of opinion that they were made in an Ushak workshop during the sixteenth and seventeenth centuries. These workshops or manufactories were weaving rugs for Western markets, a fact which many believe is confirmed by the two Centurione-Doria rugs which have the 'Lotto' designs. One of these is in the Metropolitan Museum, New York, and the other in the Kunst und Gewerbe Museum, Hamburg. Both of these rugs bear the arms of the Centurione and Doria families of Genoa. We have not seen the weave pattern of these rugs and so cannot confirm that they were made in Ushak.

An interesting observation on the 'Lotto' rugs is made by Erdmann who points out that 'Degeneration of design, so frequent in late examples of other groups, hardly ever occurs. Apparently the Lotto carpets disappeared as suddenly at the end of the seventeenth century as they had appeared at the beginning of the sixteenth.'[85]

LOURS *Persian*
See Lurs.

LULÉ *Persian*
This term was used by dealers to describe rugs that were so tightly and compactly woven that they could not be folded but had to be rolled. The word is a corruption of the French 'rouler', meaning 'to roll'.

LURI-BAKHTIAR *Persian*
This name has been used for rugs, made by the Lur tribe, with Bakhtiari designs.

LURISTAN *Persian*
See Lurs.

LURS (LUR, LURISTAN, LOURS, LORI)
Persian, Map: G6/G7
The Lur tribe led a semi-nomadic life in the Zagros Mountains, south of Kermanshah and north of Shiraz. Their production of rugs was never large and seems now to have waned to insignificance. In the trade they have also been known as Behbehan and Kalardasht, both marketing towns.

MACHLIÇ *Anatolian, Map, see Mihaliççik: C3*
Old rug name for the products of Mihaliççik.

MADEN (MADHEN) *Anatolian*
Twentieth-century rugs produced in the town of that name situated south-west of Kayseri.

MADRAS *Indian*
Modest rugs have been made here for at least a century.

MAFRASH (MAFRESH) *Caucasian and Turkoman*
The term is used in two ways: firstly, to describe a large Caucasian bag with end and side panels, making it box-shaped; and secondly, according to Azadi[86] it is the Turkoman word for a bag, also called a 'kap', which is narrower than a torba, and appears to be used only by Turkoman women.

MAHAJIRAN (MAHADSHIRAN) *Persian*
This name is mentioned by Edwards as being a weaving village in the Arak (Sultanabad) area which is 'reputed to produce the best Saruks in the whole province'.[87] Jacoby[88] gives the name as a rug name. He says the Mahajiran is a fine class of Sultanabad carpet which was made in the 1920s for the U.S.A. market. The pile is much longer than the majority of the rugs from the area, a feature which better enabled them to withstand the chemical washing to which they were subjected in order to soften the colours. It appears that the pile was deliberately made long for that reason.

As a rug name it appears to have vanished but we believe that the name 'Manchester Kashan', found only in the U.S.A. market, may well be a written or verbal corruption of Mahajiran. The Manchester Kashans we have seen would be called Sarouks outside of the U.S.A.; they are long piled and were made in the Sultanabad area.

MAHAL *Persian*
This name is an attribution of the rug trade and has little, if anything, to do with provenance other than that all Mahals come from the Sultanabad weaving area. Prior to the invasion of the area by Western entrepreneurs, two grades were recognized by the trade, namely the Mushkabads and the Mahals, the latter being the better of the two. Since the expansion of the weaving industry in the area in the 1880s a third, superior grade was added, the so-called 'Sarouk', and this is the grade commonly known in the West. Since its advent the Mushkabads and Mahals have largely been relegated to the humble status of bazaar carpets. See Feraghan.

MAHREB
Knotted rug from North Africa.

MAKATLIK *Anatolian*
Turkish word for a runner.

MAKRI (MEGRI) *Anatolian, Map, see Megri: A4*
This seaport, today called Fethiye, stands on the ancient Lycian city of Temessus which dates from the fifth century B.C. It is an active market town for the rugs made in the surrounding areas. These rugs were at one time believed to have been made on the offshore islands and were called 'Rhodian' after the principal island, Rhodes.

In 1923 the name of the harbour was changed to Fethiye and in theory the Makri rugs are those from this area, made prior to 1923, and the Fethiyes are those made subsequently. The addition of Fethiye to the world's thesaurus of rug names is inescapable, as is also the probability of a heated dispute in some distant corner as to whether a piece is a Makri, a Fethiye, or a Rhodian.

Some authorities have combined Makri and Melaz (Milâs) rugs as one group but a distinction between the two is valid both on a design and on a structural basis. See Fethiye.

MALAKAN
See Malgaran.

MALATYA *Anatolian*
Main market town for the western part of eastern Anatolia where rugs from such villages as Zara, Şarkişla, Kangal and Kavak are sold. Kurdish work is also sold there, and very often any rug sold in that market is given the name of Malatya.

MALAYER (MALAÏR) *Persian*
See Melayer.

MALGARAN (MALAKAN)
According to Mumford, certain Caucasian and East Turkestan rugs were once sold under these names, and his explanation is worth quoting as it illustrates the way some rug names were created: 'The Malakan or Malgaran people, another element in what Leroy-Beaulieu calls "the Babel of the Caucasus", have always been and are today the carriers of the region. In the early days of rug exportation from the Caucasus, when the railroad ran only as far as Tiflis, the Malakans brought the rugs there in their four-wheeled fulgons for shipment, and no name being then forthcoming, they went out under the distorted title of Malgarans. Their coming to the West from that section led to the belief that they were made somewhere in Central Asia, and since that time the Armenian dealers have made of "Malgaran" an omnibus name for all the odds and ends of unidentified Asiatic weaving.'[89]

It looks as though there might have been some confusion between two names, one of which was Margelan, a town in East Turkestan, which at one time lent its name to rugs. The names Malgaran, Malakan and Margelan are no longer used for rugs. See Margelan.

MAMLUK *Egyptian*
These carpets are believed to have been made in Cairo after it fell to the Ottomans in 1517. Some say they should be called Ottoman, but both on a design and a structural basis they are different from the large and impressive group of carpets normally called 'Ottoman' and deserve a name of their own. See Cairene and Damascus.

MANCHESTER KASHAN *Persian*
See Kashan and Mahajiran.

MANYAS *Anatolian*
Rugs from this village near Bergama. These
are often sold as Bergama.

MARASALI *Caucasian, Map, see Maraza: H3*
See Shirvan.

MARCHEKAR *Persian*
See Murdshakar.

MARDIN *Anatolian*
Town in south-eastern Turkey where rugs are
produced. The name should not be confused
with Maden (Madhen).

MARGELAN *East Turkestan*
Town east of Kokand where rugs were traded,
and which lent its name to certain rugs at one
time. See Malgaran.

MARSULIPATAM *Indian*
City in southern India that was producing
fine rugs over two hundred years ago. The
export to Western markets waned as the rugs
deteriorated and today, few, if any, reach the
West although carpet weaving is one of the
city's main industries.

MASHHAD *Persian, Map, see Meshed: K5/L5*
See Meshed.

MASUREN
Name of knotted rugs that were once made in
East Prussia. The knotting craft was
introduced into various European countries
from at least the eighteenth century in an
attempt both to take advantage of the
increasing Western interest and to
supplement the waning supplies caused by
the Arab invasion and subsequent disorder
in Persia – as well as the internal economic
and social disruption accompanying the
decline of the Ottoman Empire. The higher
cost of labour ensured that in all of those
countries, except the Balkans, the
introduction was brief and the craft quickly
returned to its homelands.

MAURCHAQ
See Afghan.

MAURI (MORI) *Afghanistan and Pakistan*
Name used alone or as a prefix to 'Bokhara' to
describe modern rugs made in designs
derived from those of the Turkoman. See
Afghan.

MAZAR-I-SHARIF *Afghanistan, Map: N5*
See Afghan.

MAZERLIK (MAZARLIK) *Anatolian*
Turkish word for rugs reserved for funeral
rites; also 'turbelik'. See Kula.

MAZLAGHAN (MAZLEGHAN) *Persian*
Design subclassification of the Hamadan
group.

MECCA SHIRAZ *Persian*
Rugs were never made in Mecca; they were,
however, offered at the shrine by pilgrims
from all over the Islamic world. These
offerings were subsequently sold by the
mollahs, or priests, and for a short while
'Mecca rugs' were known in the West when

no more positive identification than the place of export could be made. Whether the weavings of the Shiraz area in fact predominated, or whether some ingenious dealer imagined that his stock of Shiraz rugs would sell better if they were believed to have made the holy detour, is not known. It is, however, historical fact that Mecca Shiraz rugs were well known in the West and particularly in the U.S.A. The word 'Mecca' does not appear to have been prefixed to any other rug name.

MEDJIDIEH *Anatolian*
Generally used as a suffix to the rugs of Ghiordes, Kula, Ladik and Kirshehir. According to Jacoby,[90] it was a name coined by the merchants of Istanbul to signify a prayer rug. The correct position appears to be that these rugs were named after the Sultan Abdülmecid (1839-1861) who was very interested in European and particularly French culture and introduced European design into the Turkish rug industry.

MEGRI *Anatolian*
See Makri.

MEHRIBAN (MEHREVAN, MEHRIVAN) *Persian*
Two structurally distinct types of rugs are sold under this name. The one comes from the district of Mehriban, north-west of Hamadan, and belongs to the Hamadan group. The other, to which the name is more commonly applied, comes from the village of the same name in the Heriz area and belongs to the Heriz weaving group.

MEI MEI JOSHAGAN *Persian*
See Joshagan.

MEINA *Persian*
Azerbaijan village rug of the Heriz type.

MELAYER (MALAYER, MALAÏR) *Persian, Map, see Malayer: H6*
This town and district is unique in that it has lent its name to two distinct types of rugs. This is not a case of two different places with the same name as with Mehriban, but a unique case of two different though traditional techniques of weaving being used in the same town and area. Broadly speaking, in the north-western part single-wefted rugs are made which would fall into the Hamadan group. In the south-eastern area a double-wefted technique is used.

MELAZ (MELAS, MELES, MILÂS) *Anatolian, Map, see Milas: A4, Plates 49, 50*
Rugs so named come from the area south of Izmir around the town of Milâs. The old prayer rugs from this area are distinctive. As mentioned in the entry 'Makri' there is a design and structural difference between the rugs of Makri and Melaz.

Among the modern Melaz is the Ada-Milâs made in the vicinity of Karaova.

MELLAKHIR *Persian*
Name once used in the rug trade for a Bijar.

MERKIT *Persian*
Heriz-type rug made in the village of Merkit.

MERV *Turkestan, Map: L5*
Most of the Turkoman weaving tribes were to

be found living around the oasis of Merv at one time or another and therefore a Merv rug could be the product of any one of those tribes. The term is used when no more definite classification is known. It cannot be said what features indicate a Merv origin but we are aware that research is being done at the time of writing and it is hoped that it will identify a particular dye or dyes as originating from this area.

MESHED (MASHHAD) *Persian, Map: K5/L5*
Harun-ar-Rashid, the fifth Abbasid caliph (A.D.786-809), ill-advisedly created discord in the empire by dividing it between his two sons, al-Amin and al-Ma'mun.

After Harun's death near Tus, al-Ma'mun (A.D.813-833) succeeded to the caliphate after a brief but vicious civil war. Subsequently, in an attempt to reconcile the differences between the predominantly Arab Sunnites and the Persian-orientated Shi'ites, al-Ma'mun designated as his heir Ali ar-Rida, the Shi'ite eighth imam, a descendant of Ali, and gave him his daughter in marriage.

Far from creating a reconciliation, this move aggravated the situation which resulted in an insurrection of Sunnites in Baghdad. Al-Ma'mun set out to put down the insurrection and on the way his Iranian Wazir, Fadl ibn Sahl, was murdered at Sarakhs in A.D.818. Ali ar-Rida, the heir-designate, died at Tus in the same year after succumbing to a stomach disorder which his followers, the Shi'ites, believed was the result of poison. He was interred near Harun's tomb. The Shi'ites soon revered Ali ar-Rida as a martyr and as a result of the ensuing pilgrimages to his tomb, a new city called Mashhad Arridawi arose around his mausoleum. This city supplanted the nearby and ancient city of Tus.

It has been suggested under the entry 'Khorasan' – the province of which Meshed is the capital – that the attribution of the name 'Meshed' to the finer woven and shorter-clipped rugs of Khorasan arose out of a natural inclination to ascribe the best rugs to the holy city. Although it would seem likely that the city workshops would indeed produce more refined products than the rural areas, yet there is no proof that the rugs called Meshed were made in the city. The rug name 'Meshed', then must be seen simply as a description of the finest quality of Khorasan rugs, including the Belouch.

The rugs are generally known by the spelling 'Meshed', whereas the correct transliteration of the city's name is 'Mashhad'. See Amogli, Turkibaff, Farsibaff, Khorasan and Belouch.

MESHGIN (MESHKIN, MISHKIN) *Persian*
Made in the Heriz area of north-western Iran near the U.S.S.R. border, these rugs first appeared in the West at the end of the nineteenth century and are still manufactured today.

MESROBIAN *Persian*
See Hamadan.

MIANEH *Persian, Map: H5*
A dimensional term to denote 'half'. It is also the name of a town situated halfway between Zenjan and Tabriz, a halfway house so to speak. A Mianeh-Kellei can therefore be either a small Kellei or a Kellei from the

Mianeh area.

Until the end of the nineteenth century Mianeh was renowned for its distinctive and well-made products. The name is now applied to runners made in the Hamadan style and technique.

MIHALIÇÇIK *Anatolian, Map: C3*
Rugs from the village of this name in the Eskishehir region. See Machliç.

MILAS *Anatolian, Map: A4*
See Melaz.

MIR *Persian*
Type of rug once classified under this name, now rarely used on its own. It is generally used to prefix Seraband, to describe the best quality Seraband rug. See Seraband.

MIRZAPUR (MIRZAPORE) *Indian*
Situated on the right bank of the Ganges River near Benares and Allahabad, Mirzapur has a history of rug weaving dating from the early seventeenth century. Unfortunately the competition provided by prison workshops set up in the mid nineteenth century resulted in a deteriorating quality being produced until finally the erstwhile demand from Western markets waned to insignificance. Inferior carpets are still produced there today.

MISHKIN *Persian*
See Meshgin.

MOCHTASHAN *Persian*
See Motashem and Kashan.

MOGHAN *Caucasian, Map, see Steppe*

Mugan: H4
Rugs distinctive in design and weave and generally made in a long, narrow format. They come from the Moghan Steppes between Talish in the south-east and Karabagh in the west.

MOGUL *Indian*
See Mughal.

MONGOL RUGS *Mongolian*
From Chinese paintings of the thirteenth-century Sung dynasty, there appears to be no doubt that knotted rugs were made in Mongolia at that time. Mongol rugs and saddle covers of the nineteenth and twentieth centuries have reached the West but no examples older than that seem to have survived.

MORGI *Persian*
See Afshar.

MORI *Afghanistan and Pakistan*
See Mauri.

MOSUL *Anatolian and Persian*
One cannot be specific about these rugs except to say that they were not made in the northern Iraqi town of that name. Originally, as in so many instances, the name was probably borrowed from the town where the rugs were sold. The local merchants gathered their wares from many areas such as the Hamadan district, north-western Iran and north-eastern Turkey, and therefore one must look further than the name to identify the origin of a rug called Mosul.

MOSUL KURD
See Kozan.

MOTASHEM (MONCHTASHEMI,
MOCHTASHAN, MOCHTASHEM) *Persian*
The term is used alone or in conjunction with
Kashan to describe rugs from Kashan made
with a particularly fine type of wool which
imparts a recognizable velvety feel. The
derivation of the name is discussed under the
entry 'Kashan'.

MOURCHAQ
See Afghan.

MUD *Persian*
See Khorasan.

MUDJUR (MUÇUR, MUDJAR) *Anatolian,*
Map, see Muçur: C4
Rug from the town of this name south of
Kirşehir, generally known for its old prayer
rugs. The Mudjur weave is distinctive.

MUGHAL *Indian*
This name, or its alternative form, 'Mogul', is
derived from 'Mongol' and is the name of the
dynasty founded by Babur, a descendant of
both Timur (Tamerlane) and Chagatai who
was the second son of Genghis Khan. This
dynasty ruled India from 1526 until the mid
eighteenth century.
   The Mugal Empire reached its peak of
artistic expression during the reigns of Akbar
(1556-1605) called the Great, his son Jahangir
(1605-1628) and Shah Jahan (1628-1658).
   The early Mughals brought Persian
weavers to India to start court manufactories.
It is believed that these were set up in various

parts of India, the most important being at
Lahore, Agra and Fatehpur-Sikri. Initially,
designs were freely borrowed from Persia,
mainly from Herat and Isfahan, but gradually
a distinctive design sense developed. So
skilful did the Mughal weavers become that a
few of their silk rugs show the extremely high
knot-count of 39 000 per square decimetre
(2 500 per square inch). By the use of very fine
wool, knotted onto silk warp threads, a knot
count of about half this was achieved. The
less fine carpets are generally found with a
cotton warp.
   Carpets made in India during the late
seventeenth and eighteenth centuries are
commonly known as Indo-Isfahan. The
weave pattern of a number of these carpets
that have been examined by the authors,
clearly indicates that at least some of the
weavers imported by the Mughals were from
Isfahan. This fact, combined with the
similarity of their designs to those of Isfahan
carpets of the same period, is the probable
explanation for the origin of the term
'Indo-Isfahan'. See Indo-Isfahan and Girdlers'
Carpet.

MULTAN *Indian and Pakistani*
Manufactory rugs from the town of the same
name in the Punjab Province of Pakistan,
formerly in India.

MUMTAZ *Persian*
Another name for a Mahal.

MURDSHAKAR (MURCECAR,
MARCHEKAR) *Persian*
The modern spelling of the name of this town
is 'Murcheh Khur' and it is located roughly

fifty kilometres north of Isfahan. This name refers to the best quality modern Joshagan rugs.

MUSHKABAD (MUSKABAD) *Persian*
See Sultanabad.

NAFAR *Persian*
See Khamseh Confederation and Niriz.

NAIN (NA'IN, NAYEN) *Persian, Map, see Na'in: 17, Plates 51, 52*
Town one hundred and fifty kilometres north-east of Isfahan where rug knotting began in the 1930s. Despite the absence of a rug tradition, a very sophisticated industry has developed there and the standard Nain weave is finer than any other modern Persian. Technically these rugs cannot be faulted.

NAKSHA-I-GASHTA *Afghanistan*
Name meaning 'changed design' and referring to modern designs in Afghan rugs. See Afghan.

NAMAK DAN *Persian*
Qashqa'i word for a salt bag.

NAMASEH (NAMASE)
Generally namazliks or prayer rugs are of similar size, one that is easily portable. Not surprisingly the trade has adopted the word 'namaseh' as a dimensional term to describe any rug of roughly 61 cm by 122 cm (2ft by 4ft). See Joi-namaz and Namazlik.

NAMAZLIK (NAMAZLYK)
Word used for a prayer rug. It is derived from the Turkish 'namaz', meaning 'a prayer'. See Joi-namaz.

NANI *Persian*
According to Hubel[91] this is a small carpet used by the Qashqa'i as a hammock or cradle.

NEYRIZ *Persian, Map: 18*
See Niriz.

NIGDE *Anatolian, Map: C4*
This town's strategic locality has ensured its importance for centuries. Some authorities believe it to be the site of ancient Nakida which was mentioned in Hittite texts. Today it is an active market town connected by rail to all the main centres in Turkey. It has not only lent its name to rugs made in the surrounding areas but it also provides the main market for rugs from such centres as Bor, Fertek, Konya and Yesilhisar.

'THE NIGDE CARPET' *Caucasian*
So called because it was discovered at the beginning of the twentieth century in a mosque in Nigde, eastern Anatolia. The Metropolitan Museum of Art in New York, in which it now hangs, dates it from the early seventeenth century and classifies it among the early Kuba carpets of the Caucasus.

NING H'SIA *Chinese*
A carpet that bears this name is one that purports to come from the northern Chinese town or province of the same name, but as Lorenz points out, Ning H'sia acquired a connotation of quality and is commonly used for any 'well-made Chinese rug of traditional character and silky wool'.[92]

111

NIRIZ (NEYRIZ) *Persian, Map, see Neyriz: I8, Plates 53, 54*
Town about one hundred and sixty kilometres south-east of Shiraz. Several authorities have classified the rugs from this area as the work of the Afshar tribe; others attribute them to the Qashqa'i, and some say they are a peripheral Shiraz type. The Niriz weave has some affinity with all three but is nevertheless more remote from Afshar work than from the other two types. Furthermore, the Afshar are a long way east of Niriz. It would appear that either the Baharlu or the Nafar – the two predominant tribes in the Niriz area and members of the Khamseh Confederation – were the more probable weavers of the nineteenth and early twentieth-century rugs that we know as Niriz. See Laristan and Khamseh Confederation.

NOBARAN *Persian*
See Hamadan.

NOMADI *Persian*
See Qashqa'i.

O BRUK *Anatolian*
Rugs and kelims by this name are made both in the village of Obruk near Konya and by Yürüks in the surrounding area. See Kayseri and Konya.

ODJALIK (ODJAKLIK) *Anatolian*
This name has been used to denote a hearth rug, a rug with opposing mihrabs and also a prayer rug. The name is not used much, perhaps because of the confusion regarding its meaning.

OGURJALIS *Turkoman, Map: J4/J5*
See Yomut.

ORIENTAL TABRIZ
Name under which modern Romanian rugs with Oriental designs are sold in Western markets. Their weave pattern is quite distinct from the authentic Tabriz rugs.

ORTAKOY *Anatolian*
Modern rugs are produced in the northern Turkish town of this name. These are sold in Kayseri.

OSBEG *Turkestan*
See Uzbek.

OSMULDUK *Turkoman*
Decorative pentagonal panel which hangs from the side of a camel. These seem to have been made only by the Yomut. Thompson points out that the correct transliteration of the Turkic word is 'asmalik'.[93]

OTTOMAN *Anatolian*
The Ottoman Empire was founded by Osman Gazi (1258-1326) who, according to tradition, gained independence from the Sultans of Konya in 1299, the accepted founding date of the Ottoman Sultanate. It is generally believed that the name 'Ottoman' is a Western corruption of 'Osman', which in turn is a Turkish form of the Arabic 'Uthman'. Geoffrey Lewis believes that the more likely explanation is that it is derived from the purely Turkish name, 'Toman', 'which was piously but incorrectly assimilated to the Arabic name of the third successor of the Prophet [the Caliph Ottman]'.[94]

When applied to carpets, the name 'Ottoman' may be used to cover the entire period from the fourteenth to the nineteenth century, but it tends rather to be used for the period from the fourteenth to the seventeenth century. As this includes possibly the greatest period, or at least one of the greatest, in carpet history – both as a time period and because of the scale and variety of the production – it is subdivided into types described largely in terms of their designs or town of manufacture. The most famous manufacturing centres of this time were Ghiordes, Kula, Ushak, Bergama and probably Smyrna and Brusa. Some design categories are the 'Holbeins', 'Lottos' and animal rugs. See entries under these names and those of the manufacturing centres.

OUSHAK *Anatolian*
See Ushak.

Pak bokhara
An abbreviation of 'Pakistani Bokhara', otherwise called Mori. See Mori and Lahore.

PALAS
Name of a flatweave technique. Various authorities have endeavoured to draw a distinction between 'kelim' and 'palas' but without success. The following, by Landreau and Pickering, may be of assistance: 'Kilim is usually considered Turkish, palas usually something other than Turkish. Actually, palas is often used as a synonym for "Shirvan Kilim" or for large Turkoman brocaded covers. However, in Turkish, palas means literally "coarse textile rag". Kilim is a more specific term, and considering the confusion surrounding palas, would seem to be preferable for descriptive purposes.'[95]

PANDERMA (PANDERRUM) *Anatolian, Map, see Bandirma: B3, Plates 55, 56*
Rugs have been made in this town in northern Turkey near Istanbul since the late eighteenth century. According to Hubel,[96] the name is also used in the trade to describe silk rugs of the best quality from Kayseri. Many of the old Pandermas are copies of antique Ghiordes and Kula designs and many are artificially aged in an endeavour to complete the deception. However, a comparison between Plate 55 (Panderma), Plate 21 (Ghiordes) and Plate 45 (Kula) will show the patent difference between the three weaves. It is to be noted that a weave which is unusual for the place of purported origin is often the only means of detecting a forgery or misdescription.

PANGE-RANGH *Persian*
Term used by Eastern dealers to describe Kashans and Sennehs made with silk warp threads which are arranged in five bands of differing colours.

PANJDEH
See Pendeh.

PAOTOU *Chinese*
This town is the capital of the northern Chinese province of Suiyuan. Both Paotou and Suiyuan are used as rug names but Paotou rugs are distinctive in style and colouring. See Kansu.

PARDAH

In Iranian and Urdu this means a 'veil' or 'curtain' and hence 'purdah' is a curtain to screen women from the sight of men or strangers. O'Bannon[97] points out that 'pardah' is the word used in Afghanistan for a door-hanging. Academically the word should be used in place of the commonly used 'hatchli' or 'katchli' which are variations of an Armenian word for a cross, originally introduced into the vernacular of the trade as a design, not as a functional, description.

PARIZI *Persian*
See Afshar.

PAZYRYK CARPET

This was unearthed in Kurgan V near Pazyryk in the Altai Mountains of Central Asia. The Russian anthropologist in charge of the excavations, S.I. Rudenko,[98] believed that the kurgan, meaning 'barrow' dated from between the third and sixth centuries B.C.

Originally there was some doubt as to whether this was a knotted carpet. Some believed that it had been made in the cut-loop technique. It has been established beyond question that it is true knotted work made with the symmetrical knot, in a density of 3 600 knots per square decimetre.

The Pazyryk enjoyed the position of being the oldest extant example of knotted carpet work for a very short time. At Bashadar, some one hundred and eighty kilometres west of Pazyryk, a fragment of a carpet was unearthed by Rudenko which is at least a hundred and seventy years older than the Pazyryk with twice the knot density. Possibly even more interesting is the fact that, unlike the Pazyryk, the Bashadar was made with the asymmetrical knot.

We find it very interesting and most gratifying that Rudenko, an anthropologist and not a rug student, should consider that photographs of the back of both the pieces were necessary for the proper description and illustration of these finds.

Rudenko concludes from the evidence he submits, that the Pazyryk was made in Persia. Nejat Diyarbekerli,[99] Professor of Art History at the Academy of Fine Arts in Istanbul, who has made a special study of the Pazyryk Carpet, suggests that an origin nearer to where it was found may be more likely.

PENDEH (PINDE, PENDIQ, PUNJDEH, PANJDEH) *Turkoman, Map: L5/M5*

This oasis on the Murgab River was inhabited by groups of Salor, Saryk and Tekke tribesmen at different times after the beginning of the eighteenth century. Therefore the description 'Pendeh rug' is not adequate used on its own. All the Pendeh rugs have a distinctive liver-red colour and for this reason alone they are described as Pendeh in the rug trade. Apparently the dye source which produced this particular range of reds was abundantly available around the Pendeh oasis. Not all these rugs were made by one tribe, a fact that should be indicated where possible when describing one of these pieces, by suffixing the tribe's name to the word Pendeh.

PENDIN *Turkoman*
This name, as also Tekin (Tekkin), is a twentieth-century creation originating in the

114

U.S.S.R. and refers to rugs made around the Murgab oasis.

PEREPEDIL *Caucasian, Map: H3*
See Daghestan and Kuba.

PETAG *Persian*
Abbreviation of 'Persische Teppich-Aktiengesellschaft', a German company which operated a successful manufactory in Tabriz from the latter part of the nineteenth century until the early 1920s. Its products were called 'Petag rugs'.

PILLAR RUGS *Chinese and Chinese Turkestan*
Rugs made to be wrapped round pillars. They lack side borders and are made so that only when the two sides meet, can the design be seen in completion.

PINDE
See Pendeh.

POLISH RUGS
Knotted in Poland during the eighteenth century either by Persian weavers or their pupils. These rugs are not related to the genre known as 'Polonaise'.

'POLONAISE' *Persian*
In 1878 a collection of silk knotted rugs was exhibited at the Universal Exposition in Paris. As they belonged to Prince Czartoryski of Poland it was therefore incorrectly assumed that they had been made in that country. The consensus of expert opinion now accepts that they were made in Kashan and Isfahan during the late sixteenth and the seventeenth centuries, in fact, during and

after the reign of Shah Abbas. The name 'Polonaise' lingers on to describe the surviving examples which are grouped according to their design and colour.

Most of the Polonaise group of rugs have some design elements worked in metal thread. A few are made entirely in the tapestry technique but are included in the group even though they are not piled rugs.

'PORTUGUESE' RUGS *Persian*
Group of seventeenth-century carpets, so named because of their design which depicts what are believed to be Portuguese ships. For this reason the carpets were originally thought to have come from Portuguese Goa.

That attribution is no longer accepted and they are now believed to have been made in Persia. Opinion is still divided as to which part of Persia produced them, Erdmann[100] favouring the north, other authorities the south.

PRINCESS BOKHARA *Turkoman*
See Bokhara.

PUNJDEH
See Pendeh.

PUSHTI *Turkic*
A small knotted bag which can be used for a cushion. It is also a dimensional term for a piece roughly 61 cm by 98 cm (2ft by 3ft). An interesting variation on this use of the word is found among the Bugti – a tribe of the Baluchi – and is described by Sylvia Matheson as '. . . a most versatile piece of cloth'. It is used as a shawl to keep out the cold, the dust and the sand; as a pillow, sheet

or prayer-mat. A little tent can be formed by draping the pushti over a gun stuck in the ground. More remarkably, a Bugti can make himself '. . . a very comfortable "rocking-chair" with his pushti by folding it into a long strip, sitting on the ground with his knees drawn up and twisting the pushti under his armpits, around his back, then crossing the ends in front across his stomach and twisting them round his shins in a figure eight, tying the ends. Thus his back is supported and he can sit comfortably for hours.'[101]

QA'IN (CAYN, KAIN) *Persian, Map, see Qain: K7*
See Khorasan.

QALAI ZAL
See Afghan.

QALI *Persian*
See Khali.

QAJAR *Persian*
Very occasionally used to describe rugs made during the reign of the Qajar dynasty (1779-1925).

QARA CHAHI *Persian*
See Qashqa'i.

QASHQA'I (GASHGAI, KASHKAI) *Persian, Map: 18, Plates 57, 58*
Confederacy comprising the tribes of the Amaleh, Darrehshuri, Farsimadan, Keshkuli Bozarg, Shesh Boluki, Keshkuli Kuchek, Qara Chahi or Qara Chahilu, Safi Khani and Nomadi. They are mainly Turkic in origin, but over the centuries people of other ethnic origins such as Arabs, Kurds, and Lurs have been absorbed and assimilated into the confederacy and as a result have lost their separate ethnic identity.

According to J.A. Boyle[102] the Qashqa'i owe their name to Jani Agha Qashqa'i who was appointed chief of the confederacy by Shah Abbas the Great (1587-1629). Oberling,[103] on the other hand, says that the earliest-known leader was Amir Ghazi Shahilu Qashqa'i, an ancestor of Jani Agha.

The etymology of the name 'Qashqa'i' is also not clear. Various theories are proffered by the tribes themselves but there is no agreement on the origin of the word among either students or the tribes. One of the most appealing theories is that the name is derived from 'qashqa', a Turkic word which means 'a horse with a white blaze'. According to this theory the Qashqa'i believed that a horse of that description brought luck to its rider; the superstition resulted in the people being referred to as 'the people of the horses with the white spots on their foreheads'.

The tribes still lead a life which is described as semi-nomadic but more correctly it would be called a life of transhumance, as their movements are confined to seasonal migrations between predetermined winter and summer quarters in the province of Fars.

The rugs of the Qashqa'i are generally recognizable by their particular use of design. They can also be identified by weave pattern, a feature that enables them to be distinguished from imitative products made in the neighbouring Khamseh Confederation. The best old Qashqa'i rugs

116

were made by the Shesh Boluki and Keshkuli tribes. The Darrehshuri, whose seasonal migrations are to the north and south of Behbehan, appear to be the only tribe in Fars who produce the Gabeh, a coarse rug of undyed wool.

Qashqa'i designs are more akin to those of the Caucasus than to those of Persia, and this is attributed by the Qashqa'i themselves to the believed sojourn of their forebears in Azerbaijan on their way south from the ancestral Turki homelands in Central Asia.

QASVIN *Persian*
See Kasvin.

QAZAN
See Afghan.

QIZILAYAQ *Turkoman*
See Kizil Ayak and Afghan.

QULUKHTEPE-I
See Afghan.

QULYAHI *Persian*
See Kurdish.

QUM (GOUM, KOUM, KUM) *Persian, Map: I6, Plates 59, 60*
Apart from the important Shi'ite shrine of Fatima, sister of Ali ar-Rida, the martyr of Meshed, a number of other mausoleums of importance are situated in and around Qum. But it is also significant because it is situated at the crossroads linking other major cities.

The weaving industry began in Qum in the 1930s when looms were set up by a number of Kashan merchants. One of the reasons for the late appearance of the craft was the lack of wool from the immediate surroundings. Since then the manufactories have achieved renown as the producers of one of the twentieth-century genre of Persian rugs. Even more should they be acclaimed for having developed a style of their own, an achievement which is unique in the modern industry.

F.R. Martin's work provides an illustration of a rug which requires some comment; his caption is, 'A silk, decorated with Persian flowers and the lion of St. Mark. Kum about 1650.'[104] This attribution is questionable for several reasons; firstly, the mausoleums and shrines in Qum include a number of carpets dated to the seventeenth century but none of them was made in Qum; secondly, there is no reason why a Muslim should depict the lion of St Mark, and there is even less reason for decorating a Muslim shrine with a Christian symbol. The lion as a symbol of majesty, courage and bravery, enjoys a long Persian tradition – as exemplified by the lions of Persepolis and the tribal lion-rugs of Fars. The lion in Martin's illustration was certainly not the lion of St Mark, but may have been the lion of Ali ibn Abi Talib, the fourth Caliph, called the 'lion of God'.

The Qum weavers use many designs, some original, some adaptations of designs from other areas. Among the latter group we have discovered a type of rug described as a 'Jozandi Qum' which is intended to signify a Qum with a Jozan design.

RAHATY *Persian*
Village rug of the Hamadan type.

117

RAVAR *Persian*
See Kerman.

RHODES (RHODIAN) *Anatolian*
See Makri.

ROYAL BOKHARA *Turkoman*
See Bokhara.

RUPALANI *Persian*
Also called 'gashya', meaning 'a saddle cover'.

RUSSIAN BOKHARA
See Bokhara.

RUTAKALI *Persian*
Horse rug.

SAARABAD *Persian*
See Afshar.

SABZAWAR (SABZAVAR, SABZEVAR, SABSAVAR, SABSUVAR) *Persian and Belouch, Map, see Sabzavar: K6*
The master-spelling of this word is that used by the National Geographic Society for both of two very distinct rug producing villages. The one is located about one hundred and seventy kilometres west of Meshed where good quality rugs of the Khorasan type are produced. The second village is about one hundred and thirty kilometres south of Herat and produces, or used to produce, rugs which Clark included in his 'South-Western Afghanistan Group'.[105] This group is also referred to by Dilley[106] who, like Clark, uses the spelling 'Sabzwar'. They both say that the name means 'green coloured'. Today these 'Sabzwar' rugs would generally be included in the Belouch group.

SAFAVID *Persian*
Name used to describe carpets made during the reign of the Safavid dynasty (1501-1736). The capital of Persia was moved from Herat to Tabriz and these two cities – as well as Kashan, Isfahan and Kerman – became famous as centres of art, including the weaving of textiles and carpets. Over one thousand carpets have survived from this period, and they include the most splendid examples of the Persian carpet art.

SAFI KHANI *Persian*
See Qashqa'i.

SAIDABAD *Persian*
Town in south-western Iran where Afshar rugs are marketed. The name is also used for the finest quality Afshars.

SAJJADA
Arabic word for a prayer rug. See Sejadeh.

SALATCHAK *Turkoman*
Hexagonal rug roughly 122 cm by 61 cm (4ft by 2ft), with the pattern of the prayer arch, and used as a cradle. These rugs have been mistakenly described as prayer rugs, but in this case the mihrab – the prayer arch – is included as symbolical protection for the child.

SALIANI (SAL'YANY) *Caucasian, Map, see Sal'yany: H4*
See Baku.

SALOR *Turkoman, Map: L6, Plates 61, 62*
Knowledge of Turkoman history prior to the seventeenth century is based largely on the writings of Mahmud Kashghari who wrote in the eleventh century, and Rashid al-din in the thirteenth century. According to both authors, the Turkoman tribes all claim the legendary Oghuz Khan as their primogenitor.

Since the eleventh century some tribes have disappeared and others have come into existence but the Salor remain one of the few tribes listed by both Mahmud Kashghari and Rashid al-din as comprising the original twenty-four Turkoman clans. Until the early part of the nineteenth century the Salor were the pre-eminent Turkoman tribe. Their importance is illustrated by some of the newer tribes claiming a Salor as their founder and by early geographical distribution of the tribe being reported in relation to the Salor. According to *The Genealogy of the Turkoman*, written by Abul-Ghazi Bahadur, Khan of Khiva in the middle of the seventeenth century, only the Saryk and Tekke are justified in claiming descent from the Salor.

Abul-Ghazi refers to the 'Stone Salor' who existed in Khorasan in the early sixteenth century, and says that the name included the Saryk, Yomut, Tekke and Ersari. Other writers have also referred to the 'Inner' and 'Outer' Salor. One understands from Jani-Mahmud Ghujdurvani, who wrote in the sixteenth century, that the Inner Salor lived on the coast of the Caspian Sea, and the Outer Salor were those who lived further east towards Khiva. The same terminology is found in the writings of Abul-Ghazi who refers to the more southerly Salor as being divided into the Inner Salor (those of

Khorasan) and the Outer (those to the east, comprising the Tekke, Saryk and Yomut). At that time Khorasan comprised an area far larger than the present Iranian province and included Merv and Herat.

The Turkoman people migrated south over many centuries due to pressures both from the Khazaks and from each other, and because of the drying up of the Uzboy water system. At the beginning of the nineteenth century the main body of the Salor was located around Serakhs. They had been under pressure for some time from the Saryk who in turn were moving south as the result of pressure from the Tekke who had by then become the dominant tribe in Turkmenia.

The fortunes of the Salor were on the wane and they ceased to be a significant tribe following their defeat by the Persian army under Abbas Mirza who led a two-year campaign in 1831 in retribution and reprisal for the constant Turkoman raids. At some stage in this part of their history, the Salor ceased weaving rugs. It is not certain whether this was a result of their crushing defeat or because, as Bogolyubov reported, 'the Persian Khans, when they became their [the Salor's] new masters, confiscated all their better products and more or less forced them to give up their traditional occupation'.[107] It is beyond dispute that their guls and designs, but not their individual and subtle use of colour, lived on in the weavings of other tribes. Their weave patterns disappeared, but many rugs and bags were made and are still being made with the Salor designs; the weave patterns of these pieces are not of the Salor.

The weave pattern illustrated in Plate 61 is that of the old Salor fragment owned by the

Museum of Fine Arts, Boston. This same weave pattern is to be seen in other surviving Salors of which the Victoria and Albert Museum, London has several. This weave pattern appears to have ceased suddenly as not one of the late nineteenth and twentieth-century rugs, so often described as Salor, is made in the same way.

'SALTING CARPET' *Anatolian*
This was part of the Salting Collection and is now in the Victoria and Albert Museum, London, but it alone acquired sufficient notoriety to be labelled the 'Salting Carpet'. Originally it was described as a sixteenth-century Persian carpet but its genealogy and age were put in question and it is now believed to have been made in Istanbul no earlier than the eighteenth century.

SALTOQ
See Afghan.

SAMAN *Persian*
See Bakhtiari.

SAMARKAND *East Turkestan, Map: N4*
This very ancient and important city on the Silk Road was occupied by many different powers including Alexander the Great, the Arabs, the Persian Samanids and various Turkic groups. It was destroyed by Genghis Khan but rebuilt in the fourteenth century by Tamerlane under whose reign were constructed some of its most remarkable buildings.

As a major city of Central Asia, it was an important market and earlier this century its name was used to describe all rugs from eastern Central Asia, including those which are now generally called Khotan, Kashgar and Yarkand.

There is a type of coarsely knotted modern rug sold under the name of Samarkand.

SAMUCH-GENDJE *Caucasian*
Design subdivision of Gendje rugs.

SANGUSZKO CARPETS *Persian*
Group of Shah Abbas (1587-1629) medallion carpets which take their name from the one in the collection of Prince Roman Sanguszko in Paris. This particular rug was first exhibited in Leningrad in 1904.

SAPH (SAFF)
Name for the multiple prayer-rug or family prayer-rug. These rugs include three or more prayer divisions each with its own mihrab. Production appears to have been confined to Turkey, East Turkestan and Mughal India. Large saphs are found in mosques in Turkey.

SARAB (SIRAB) *Persian, Map: H5*
Town between Tabriz and Ardebil. The rugs now known as Sarabs are long and narrow in shape. Formerly, rugs of a fine quality from this area were known as 'Serapi' ('Serape') but the name is seldom heard nowadays even by the dealers who were accustomed to use the names in their youth.

SARAKS (SERAKHS) *Persian*
See Bijar.

SARAND *Persian*
Weaving village near Tabriz which produces

rugs of the Tabriz type and is not to be confused with 'Zarand', a type of Kerman. The use of the name 'Sarand' is very limited and is one of the many examples of attributing a specific design feature to a village, which may or may not be the place of origin or even the exclusive place of manufacture of that design.

SARD RUD *Persian*
Hamadan village rug.

SARIQ
See Saryk.

ŞARKIŞLA *Anatolian*
See Malatya.

SAROOQI
See Afghan and Saryk.

SAROUK (SARUK) *Persian, Map, see Saruk: H6, Plates 63, 64, 65, 66*
This village produced exceptionally good rugs which were made for a relatively short period up to the end of the nineteenth century. Their virtues were extolled wherever they were known and their early demise was a cause for universal regret. In memoriam, the name lives on as a label for the best quality rugs from the Sultanabad weaving complex. Unfortunately, like all memorials, only the name, not the quality or characteristics is perpetuated. One reputed feature of the old Sarouks is preserved – whether fortuitously or knowingly, is a matter for speculation – and that is the weft colour. At least one early authority referred to the distinctive blue weft of the Sarouks, and as

a result, modern 'Sarouks' have a blue weft. But an examination of original Sarouks will show that a blue weft was in fact unusual. The common weft was undyed cotton though some old Sarouks are to be found with a weft of a very pale bluish hue.

Plates 63 and 64 illustrate an old Sarouk, and Plates 65 and 66 a Sultanabad 'Sarouk'. See Sultanabad.

SARYK (SARIQ, SAROOQI) *Turkoman, Map: L5/M5 Plates 67, 68*
One of the tribes which have lived around Merv, Pendeh and Yuletan since the early nineteenth century. Their name appears in historical literature during the fifteenth and sixteenth centuries though they may well have been an autonomous group prior to that. Neither Mahmud Kashghari nor Rashid al-din mentions the Saryk in their lists of Oghuz clans. Most of the rugs which the trade describes as Pendeh, are the work of the Saryk; this statement is based on the study of their weave patterns. The authors also hold the view that a number of the so-called 'Kizil Ayak' door-hangings, or engsi, were in fact made by the Saryk and not the Kizil Ayak tribe. See Kizil Ayak.

Folklore would have us believe that the Salor taught the Saryk to weave and they in turn taught the Tekke. Whether this was so or not can never be established but there is a superficial similarity between the weave pattern of the late nineteenth-century Saryk rugs and that of the old Salors. This similarity has misled at least one authority, yet little more than a cursory examination will show a definite difference between the two techniques.

SAUJBULAGH *Persian*
See Sujbulagh.

SAVALANS *Persian*
See Sultanabad.

SAVEH *Persian*
See Hamadan.

'SAVONNERIE'
During the nineteenth century when the products of this factory in Paris had reached a peak of popularity the knotting craft in Persia had reached a state of dire depression. In an attempt to revitalize interest, a number of Persian weaving centres – especially Kerman – began to make carpets in designs that were taken from Savonnerie carpets.

SCHMIEDEBERGER
Hand-knotted carpets were made in Silesia from the middle of the nineteenth century for about sixty years. Those made in Schmiedeberger received the most acclaim and were exported to the U.S.A. for a period.

SECCADE *Anatolian*
See Sejadeh.

SEFIABAD *Persian*
Hamadan area village rug.

SEJADEH
Dimensional term for a rug measuring approximately 122 cm by 213 cm (4ft by 7ft). The Turkish equivalent is 'seccade'. These words both appear to be derived from the Arabic word 'Sajjada' meaning 'prayer rug'.

SELÇUK *Anatolian*
There are several Turkish villages of this name. Rugs of the Konya type are made in the nearby village of Selçuk and are sometimes known as Konya Selçuk. See Kayseri and Konya.

SELJUK (SELJUG) *Anatolian*
Beginning in the late tenth century and ending in the latter half of the thirteenth century, the Seljuks – who stemmed from a ruling family of one of the Central Asian Turkoman clans – ruled an Empire that included Mesopotamia, Asia Minor, Syria and Persia. Professor Oktay Aslanapa says that 'the Seljuks brought their knowledge of weaving with them from Central Asia where they are known to have been making carpets since before the third century A.D.'[108] The largest collection of Seljuk rugs and fragments of rugs, which were made in Anatolia, is preserved in the Turkish Islamic Arts Museum in Istanbul. In spite of the great changes that took place in the designs of carpets made in Anatolia under the Ottomans who succeeded the Seljuks, some design motifs from the Seljuk period are still being used in the nomad and village rugs of Anatolia today.

SELVILE *Persian*
Mumford[109] recorded a type of rug of this name known to Turkish and U.S.A. dealers at the time when he wrote. He said the Selvile was no more than a coarse Seraband.

SEMNAN (SAMNAN) *Persian*
Town one hundred and seventy kilometres east of Tehran where the weaving of rugs is a

122

recent occupation. Copies of old Isfahan designs are made.

SENDSHAN *Persian*
See Zenjan.

SENNEH (SEHNA, SENNA, SINNEH)
Persian, Map: G6, Plates 69, 70
This town is now called Sanandaj, and is situated north-west of Hamadan and south of Bijar in the heart of what is unofficially called Persian Kurdistan. The granular feel of the Senneh weave is unique and one can often identify it by feel alone. In appearance and feel the weave is quite different from that of the Bijar and from the other Kurdish weaves.

Senneh has been famous for its finely woven rugs and kelims for at least two hundred years.

No one seems to know why Senneh has given its name to the asymmetrical, open, or Persian knot, but the name continues to be used despite the fact that the use of this knot by the Senneh weavers is very rare.

SERABAND (SARABAND, SERABEND)
Persian, Map: H6
The weavers of the Sarawan district of Iran have adhered to a traditional design far more rigorously than those of any other weaving district. Concerning the rugs of Seraband, that is probably the only statement on which all authorities would agree. It is accepted that 'Seraband' is a corruption of 'Sarawan', but the origin of the name 'Mir' – generally prefixed to 'Seraband' – is obscure. Whether or not there was at one time a Mir rug from this area is also not clear, but 'Mir-Seraband' came to be used as a quality description and

it is therefore not surprising that the combination of names is more common than 'Seraband' on its own.

Mumford[110] says that Mir was the name of the village where Seraband rugs were made. This suggestion is amplified by Hawley who says 'the best of these pieces are made in the town of Mirabad, which signifies "the city of Mir", and are accordingly called Mir Sarabands'.[111] Dilley[112] adds that the town of Mir was destroyed by an earthquake. Acknowledging the doubt in derivation, Edwards submits two explanations. He says firstly, 'The origin of the name "Mir" is not easy to explain. It is probably connected with the village of Mal-e-Mir – the administrative centre of the district – but the connection is not clear. Mr. Naserullah Mostaufi of Ahwaz – an authority on the geography, manners and customs of his country – informed me that during the period when these carpets were woven, a considerable number of mirs were living in the Seraband district. The Seraband mirs – unlike most of the sayyids of Persia – were among the best elements of the population, and it was in their homes that the Mir carpets were woven. It is conceivable that the village of Mal-e-Mir (i.e. the property of the mirs) became their principal seat.'[113] Edwards's second suggestion is that they were woven to the order of a certain Emir Kabir and that 'Mir' is the corruption of 'Emir'.

Two schools of thought exist in regard to the structure of these rugs. Mumford, Hawley and Dilley say they are made with the asymmetrical knot. Eiland[114] and Edwards disagree and maintain that the symmetrical knot is invariably used. Kendrick and Tattersall[115] say they are generally made with the asymmetrical knot but that some are found with both types of knot. The authors have examined a number of antique Serabands which were all made with the asymmetrical knot but cannot vouch for the invariability of this feature. We venture to suggest that some of the Serabands with the symmetrical knot were made in Isparta and Kayseri.

Good quality carpets with the well-known all-over design of the Serabands are still being made in Iran, while inferior copies are made in Pakistan.

SERAFIAN *Persian*
Name of an Isfahan master-weaver of the twentieth century. The rugs produced in his workshop all bear his name.

SERAKHS *Persian*
See Saraks and Bijar.

SERAPI (SERAPE) *Persian*
See Sarab.

SERIN
Small cushion, probably Kurdish.

SEWAN (SEVAN) *Caucasian, Map, see Sevan: G3*
See Kazak.

SEYSHOUR (SEICHUR, SEJSHOUR, SEJUR, ZACHOUR) *Caucasian, Map: H3, Plates 71, 72*
See Kuba.

SEYSSAN *Persian*
Type of rug mentioned only by Dilley who says they were produced in 'four or five villages of Babists, located out of Tabriz on the road to Teheran'.[116]

SHADDA (SHADDAH, SHEDDA) *Caucasian*
Name of a flatwoven blanket from the Caucasus.

SHAH ABBAS *Persian*
Shah Abbas I (1587-1629), known as the Great, is considered to have been the most outstanding Safavid king because of his military successes, encouragement of the arts and because of his religious tolerance which made him the first Persian ruler to exchange embassies with a Western nation. It was as a result of these embassies that Persian carpets began to reach Europe. Although splendid wool carpets have survived from the reign of Shah Tahmasp – Abbas's predecessor who also promoted the weaving crafts – far more carpets, including many silks, have survived from Abbas's reign. It is usually said that the art of the Persian carpet, particularly in silk, reached its peak at this time when many of the famous 'hunting', 'animal', 'vase' and 'Polonaise' carpets were made. Shah Abbas is believed to have been an accomplished weaver himself and so interested was he in the art that he set up court manufactories in at least three centres during his reign.

SHAHRABIAN *Persian*
See Tabriz.

SHAHRBAFF *Persian*
See Hamadan.

SHAHRISTAN

124

Trade name used early in the twentieth century for rugs made in various places, including Bulgaria, India and Persia. The name does not seem to be used any longer.

SHAHSAVAN (SHAHSEVAN, SCHASEWEN) *Persian, Map, see Shahsevan: H5*
The Shahsavan ('faithful to the Shah') tribe lead a nomadic life in north-western Iran between Ardebil and Saveh. Some authorities have credited them with no more than the ability to sell the wool from their flocks. This is not correct; they not only weave pile carpets but also flatweaves of great merit. In his book, an illustration of a Shahsavan rug dated 1795 is provided by Carl Hopf.[117]

SHALEMGAR *Persian*
See Bakhtiari.

SHARABIAN *Persian*
See Tabriz.

SHEMAKHA *Caucasian*
See Soumak.

SHEMRAN *Persian*
Tehran orphanage where rugs were made and from which they acquired their name.

SHIBERGHAN
See Afghan.

SHIKLI *Caucasian*
See Kazak.

SHIRAZ *Persian, Map: I8*

This city has been culturally and historically important for many centuries. Two of Iran's greatest poets, Sa'di (1184-1282) and Hafez (1320-1389) were both born and buried there. It was the capital of the Zand dynasty (1750-1794) and is at present the capital of the Fars province. A school of Persian miniature painting was centred in Shiraz and reached its peak in the sixteenth century. It is the centre of a wine industry that is famous far and wide, and has given its name to a type of wine grape.

Some authorities deny that rugs were ever made in Shiraz and maintain that the use of the name for rugs is due to the fact that the surrounding nomad tribes, among them the Qashqa'i, Baharlu, Ainalu, Keshkuli, Farsimadan and Shesh Boluki, all marketed their rugs in the city.

Others assert, more convincingly, that Shiraz was an important rug-weaving centre. Indeed it would be unlikely that rugs were not made in a city that maintained its importance for many centuries and was surrounded by rug weaving people. Wherever there was wealth rugs were made and from successful commissions manufactories developed.

See Mecca Shiraz.

SHIRVAN *Caucasian, Map: H3/H4*
Regarding the classification of Caucasian rugs, many dogmatic statements are made which are not supported by the evidence. One hears that Shirvans invariably have the following distinguishing technical features: 'they always have a brown woollen warp', 'the shirazi, or edges, are always white', 'the warp threads do not lie one above the other

but almost horizontally next to one another'. These features, however, are not exclusive to Shirvan rugs. Plates 11 and 12 show an old Chi Chi with its original edges intact. The design is indisputably Chi Chi. Rugs of this type come from the Kuba area but this rug shows all three of the technical features which would supposedly identify it as a Shirvan. Is it then a Shirvan? The authors have so far met no one who would call it a Shirvan.

Schürmann[118] provides the following subdivisions of the rugs of the Shirvan area: Akstafa, Bidjov, Chajli and Marasali; the design of the latter is believed to have originated in the village of Maraza (Map: H4). These four names are all design subdivisions and there are many rugs made in the Shirvan area which do not fall into any one of these four divisions. In regard to Akstafa, although the area is geographically closer to the Kazak region than to Shirvan, technically the Akstafa rugs appear to be generally more akin to the so-called 'Shirvans' than to the Kazaks.

The Shirvan area is south of Kuba, bounded on the west by the Karabagh and Gendje areas and in the south by Baku.

The question of technical differences in the weaves of the eastern Caucasus is discussed under the entry 'Daghestan', where the point is made that one cannot be dogmatic in classifying the rugs of this region on either a design or a structural basis. There are a few named rug-types in the Caucasus which can be separately classified on structural criteria, but we do not believe the rugs that are normally labelled 'Shirvan' to be one of them. Plates 1 and 2 illustrate an Akstafa.

SHULAVER *Caucasian, Map, see Shulaveri: G3*

See Kazak.

SHUSHA *Caucasian, Map: G4*
See Karabagh.

SIEBENBURGEN *Anatolian*
See Transylvanian.

SILEH (SILÉ, ZILE)
A name of uncertain origin which is used for types of flatwoven rugs with or without some brocading. It is most commonly used for the large brocaded Caucasian rugs with a design of rows of large S-shaped figures which are believed to represent stylized dragons. The name does not appear to be a Caucasian village name. There is a village of Zile in north-central Turkey, but no connection between the two has yet been established. See Zile.

SINEKLI (SINEKLIS) *Anatolian*
Word meaning 'flies' and used to describe a design feature of small motifs covering the field in a number of Turkish rugs such as Ghiordes, Kula and Kirshehir.

SIRDAR
See Trade Names.

SISTAN (SEISTAN) *Map, see Zabol: L8*
Term which has been used for inferior Belouch rugs from Zabol and the surrounding Seistan area. Edwards[119] says that some finely woven 'balisht', or small square bags, originate here. See Belouch.

SIVAS *Anatolian*
This town is the capital of the Sivas province

126

in central Turkey, and was known in Roman times as 'Sebasteia'. This name was changed to 'Sivas' after the Seljuk conquest of that part of Anatolia in 1071. In 1919 it was the venue of a nationalist congress presided over by Mustafa Kemal (Atatürk) to organize resistance to the Allied proposal of partitioning Anatolia.

Rugs have been made there for centuries and the old rugs of Sivas were widely known and acclaimed. Unfortunately, during the twentieth century, the revival of the rug making craft in Turkey has resulted in the manufacture, in Sivas and other places, of inferior products which are generally sold as Smyrna or Sparta.

SIYAR-KAR
Several early authors record that in the East, the products of the Baluchi were called by this name which means 'dark work' and refers to the generally rather sombre colouring of Belouch rugs.

SMYRNA *Anatolian, Map: A3*
The old name for Izmir, an important seaport on the Aegean, which has been inhabited since a period contemporaneous with ancient Troy.

Although manufactories have existed there from at least the eighteenth century, the rugs of Smyrna over the past two hundred years have not had a style of their own, unless individuality can be expressed in the manner of copying designs from elsewhere. During the twentieth century it has been second only to Istanbul as a port for the export of rugs to the West. As a rug manufacturing town, it is the Sultanabad of Turkey, being entirely a commercial creation both because of its seaport and because all the materials required for rug weaving, as well as labour, are readily available.

As a market place Smyrna collected rugs from far and wide, to the extent that a number of rug centres that had maintained their own traditional designs, also began to make other designs and inferior grades specially for the Smyrna market and these were sold as Smyrna rugs. One hears of Smyrna-Feraghans, Smyrna-Serabands, Smyrna-Sivas, and even Smyrna-Sennehs – all traditional designs from other places as copied by the Smyrna suppliers. The name 'Smyrna' has had an even wider connotation, as it has been used in the rug trade as a substitute for 'Turkish' or 'Anatolian'.

SOMA *Anatolian, Map: A3*
See Bergama.

SONGUR *Persian*
Kurdish village rug from the Hamadan region.

SOUMAK *Caucasian*
Corruption of the name 'Shemakha', which was from the ninth to the sixteenth century the residence of the shahs of Shirvan. Soumak-work is a type of brocading in wool onto a flatwoven fabric, and is mostly associated with the Caucasus, though there are also Anatolian and Persian soumak pieces.

'SPANISH HOLBEIN' *Spanish*
See 'Holbein'.

SPARTA *Anatolian*
See Isparta.

'SPRING OF CHOSROES' *Persian*
King Chosroe (Khusrau) II, one of the Persian
Sassanian dynasty (A.D.224-642) was
conquered by Heraclius in A.D. 638.
Amongst the loot taken from his palace at
Ctesiphon was a fabulous carpet of immense
size and value, said to include pearls and
precious stones. It was designed to represent
a Persian garden in spring and hence its
name. Although the carpet was divided and
distributed, and no part of it survives, its
existence has been established from early
literary sources.

SRINAGAR *Indian*
Manufactory rugs from northern India.

SUIYUAN *Chinese*
See Kansu and Paotou.

SUJBULAGH (SAUJBULAGH,
SOUJ-BOULAK, SOUCH-BULAGH,
SAVOJBOLAGH) *Persian, Map, see
Saujbulagh: G5*
For a short period after the Second World
War, this city was the centre of an
autonomous Kurdish republic. The city is
now known as Mahabad. Old Sujbulagh rugs
are probably the most prized of all the
Kurdish weaves but unfortunately very few
reach Western markets.

SULEIMAN (SULIMANI)
See Afghan.

SULTAN *Anatolian or Persian*

The trade recognizes this type of rug as a
shaggy, very long-piled rug, made by Yürüks
in north-eastern Turkey or north-western
Iran.

SULTANABAD (SOLTANABAD) *Persian,
Map: H6*
This city, now called Arak, was founded in
1808 and is the hub of commercial rug
production in Iran.

Broadly speaking, the difference between
the Hamadan weaving complex and that of
Arak is that in the former area different
designs are made in different villages largely
according to tradition, whereas in Arak the
work of one village is only distinguished
from that of another by the grade, as the same
designs are produced throughout the area.

The best rugs produced are known as
Sarouks. The inferior grades are the
Mushkabads, Mahals, Araks and
Sultanabads, though which are the better and
which the worse is a matter of individual
choice, as dealers are not agreed on the
arrangement of these names on a scale of
quality. Some merchants use the names
'Savalan' and 'Sarouk-Mahal' to designate
certain qualities of Sultanabad rugs, but these
terms are meaningless to all except the dealer
who chooses to use them.

Plates 65 and 66 illustrate a modern
'Sarouk' grade of Sultanabad and a
comparison with the old Sarouk (Plates 63
and 64) will show the patent difference in
weave patterns. The modern 'Sarouk' has
borrowed the name of the original type made
in the village of Sarouk, but there is no
genealogical relationship.

When the firms of Hotz & Son and Ziegler

128

and Company organized the Sultanabad production at the end of the nineteenth century, their sole objective was to produce rugs that would meet Western demand. It is therefore not surprising that Western designers were used and that they modified traditional designs to conform with Western taste as they understood it. The result was designs that one would call Persian derivatives. It may well be that these commercial creations prolonged the life of a moribund craft, but nothing could have been contrived more surely to destroy any remaining artistic spontaneity. Some of the products of this area are no better than polychromatic floor-coverings though the best are hard wearing, and do have an appeal, though not to the traditionalist. See Mahajiran.

SURAHANI (SURAKHANY, SOURAGHAN)
Caucasian, Map, see Surakhany: H4
See Baku.

SUZANI *Turkestan*
Word derived from the Iranian 'suzan' meaning 'a needle'. It refers to a type of large, Central Asian embroidery using silk thread on a cotton base. These beautiful, floral pieces were made as hangings and bed-covers and are the work of Uzbeks living in the towns of Bokhara, Samarkand, Nurata and Tashkent among others. These people also produced a variety of smaller embroidered pieces using several embroidery stitches, the most common being cross-stitch and chain-stitch.

TABA TABAIE *Persian*
See Tabriz.

TABRIZ *Persian, Map: G4, Plates 73, 74*
The story of this city is one of repeated destruction, survival, restoration and revival. In A.D. 791 it was rebuilt after a devastating earthquake. It rose again after major earthquakes in A.D. 858, 1041, 1721 and 1780. It survived the invasions of the Mongols, Tamerlane, the Ottomans and the Afghans. It also survived two Russian occupations, one in 1827 and the other under Stalin's regime in 1941.

Arab historians record that Tabriz was an important rug-weaving centre as early as the time of Harun-ar-Rashid. (See Meshed.) Some of the most artistic expressions of the sixteenth-century Persian craft were produced in Tabriz. However, from the time of the Afghan invasion in 1722 until the late nineteenth century, the manufactories ceased to exist and the craft returned to the level of the village weaver making no more than sufficient for his own needs.

At the end of the nineteenth century three inspired Persian master-weavers, Hajji Jalil, Sheik Safi and Kurban Dai were the flames of revival sparked by an ever-increasing demand from Western markets. Of this trio, Hajji Jalil was probably the most renowned and is best known for his silk carpets. He was followed by other master-weavers such as Jahfer and Jowan. The mid twentieth century has seen the rise in the fortunes of yet another master-weaver, Taba Tabaie. His rugs are very popular in the U.S.A. where they are affectionately and not uncommonly referred to as 'Taba Tabriz'.

In earlier times the rugs of Tabriz were made with the asymmetrical knot but the revival of the craft brought a general change in technique. Although this revival was initiated under the supervision of Kerman master-weavers, the products of Tabriz – unlike those of Kerman – are now made with the symmetrical knot.

Tabriz has a far greater repertoire of designs than any other weaving centre. It is true that the Tabriz workshops have borrowed traditional design features from other areas, but the manner of use is typically that of Tabriz. They have copied antique designs as well as creating new designs that are different from the traditional Persian style.

The nearby village of Koy produces rugs in the Tabriz style and technique but of coarser structure and different in colouring.

'Shahrabian' is another rug name from the Tabriz area which some place in the Heriz complex. See Sarand.

TACHTEKABI *Persian*
See Hamadan.

TAFRISH (TAFRESH) *Persian*
See Hamadan.

TAGHAN
See Afghan.

TAINAKSHA (KONAKCHA) *Caucasian and Turkoman*
Saddle rug or horse blanket, also known as an 'at-joli'.

TAJ MAHAL *Indian*
See Trade Names.

TALISH *Caucasian, Map: H4*
These rugs came from the region of the Talish Mountains in the most southern part of the Caucasus, north of Ardebil in Iran. Schürmann's[120] classification of Caucasian rugs allocates a separate class to the Talish rugs and their one subdivision, the Lenkoran. Based on all the criteria of design, provenance and structure, the Talish rugs are entitled to a separate classification.

TANTYE *Persian*
Name used in the Fars province of Iran for a small woven bag or purse carried by a shoulder strap.

TAPETI DAMASCHINI
See Damascus.

TASHPINAR (TAŞPINAR) *Anatolian*
See Konya.

TCHERKESS (CHERKESS) *Caucasian*
This illustrates yet another case where the doyens of the trade adhere to a name with conviction of its accuracy and with a shrug at modern attempts to improve the classification of Caucasian rugs. Colour, design and some structural features appear to be the criteria which set the Tcherkess apart from the so-called 'Kazaks' although their weave is indistinguishable from what is generally regarded as a Kazak weave. Tcherkess rugs were also known as Circassian, but it is generally believed that the Circassians did not make knotted rugs.

TCHETCHEN (CHECHEN) *Caucasian*
Chi Chi rugs were once known by this name.
See Chi Chi.

TEHRAN (TEHERAN) *Persian, Map: 16*
The quantity of rugs manufactured in and
around this city was never substantial and
dwindled to insignificance prior to the
Second World War. Their designs were not
traditional but their technical excellence more
than compensated for what they lacked in
genealogy.

TEHRAN QUM *Persian*
Name devised to label twentieth-century rugs
that look as if they were made in Qum, but
appear to pre-date the Qum workshops.
'Tehran', being another possibility, is added
to 'Qum' but it is a pity that the word 'or' is
not inserted between the two names to
indicate what is really intended.

TEIMURI
See Timuri.

TEKIN *Turkoman*
See Pendin.

TEKKE *Turkoman, Map: K4/K5, L5/M5, Plates
75, 76*
Neither Mahmud Kashghari nor Rashid
al-din mentions the Tekke in their lists of the
original Oghuz clans formed by the sons of
the legendary Oghuz from whom all
Turkoman claim descent.

The Tekke are believed to be an offshoot of
the Salor. This belief forms part of their oral
tradition and is recorded by foreign writers as
the Turkoman had no written language of

their own. Abul-Ghazi Bahadur, Khan of
Khiva, who wrote *The Genealogy of the
Turkoman* in 1660, associates the Tekke with
the Salor. The following excerpt from
Barthold, who quotes Abul-Ghazi, is of
interest: '. . . to the Outer Salor belonged the
tribes Teke, Sariq and Yomut. About the
origins of the Teke and Sariq the Genealogy
says that their ancestor was a certain
Toz-Tutmaz from among the Salor.'[121]

Apart from those weave patterns which
may be aberrations, hybrids or inaccurate
attributions, we can isolate two identifiable
Tekke weaves: Plate 75 illustrates one of
these.

The existence of two weave patterns in the
same ethnic group is discussed in the
monograph. As regards the Tekke, the
problem is related to the divisions and
geographical distribution of the tribe which
in itself is no easy problem to resolve. We are
dealing with a nomadic group, frequently on
the move, and, up to the time of the tribe's
conquest by the Russians at Geok Tepe in
1881, constantly at war in the ever-present
struggle for water and grazing for their herds.

From the beginning of the eighteenth
century the largest group of Tekke was to be
found around the Akhal oasis located near
Geok Tepe (Map: K5). There were smaller
groups on the Atrek River, around Merv and
on the lower reaches of the Murgab River and
in north-western Afghanistan. Apart from
the geographical distribution, there was also
the military division into the Tokhtamish and
Otamish groups. These were apparently
subdivided, the Tokhtamish group into the
Bek and Vekil, and the Otamish group into
the Bakhshi and Sytshma. In what way these

tribal subdivisions corresponded to geographical distribution is not clear. What is apparent is that groups of the same tribe were often remote from one another and sometimes even separated by a group from some other tribe. The co-existence of two weave patterns in the same tribe is therefore understandable. As we have said under the entry 'Merv', we are aware of research being done which is attempting to relate the two main types of Tekke rugs to specific areas where the Tekke are known to have lived. This research is concerned with the analysis of dyes. For the moment it is not possible to say where any particular Tekke originated.

TENT BANDS
See Kibitka.

TIBETAN CARPETS
According to Denwood, the industry is an old one going back possibly over one thousand years, and was probably learnt from the people of Central Asia; parts of that area were under Tibetan control for a long time. Central Asia has had a strong influence on Tibetan carpet weaving but since the eighteenth century, China – whose carpet industry is much younger than that of Tibet – has exercised a very considerable influence on Tibetan designs, while Buddhist design elements from India have played a part.

In older carpets, a cutloop technique was used, but this has largely given way to assymetrical and symmetrical knotting in the modern rugs. In common with the rest of the carpet weaving world, a more commercial attitude has meant that manufactories have to some extent replaced the old folkcraft. Most modern Tibetan carpets seem to be made in India, Nepal, Sikkim and Bhutan where large numbers of refugees from Communist Tibet settled in the 1950s. In Denwood's words: '. . . carpet weaving is a minor manifestation of traditional Tibetan culture and as such it probably survives in a more traditional form outside Tibet proper than inside it.'[122]

TIEBAFF *Persian*
Iranian merchants make a distinction between Meshed rugs which have no jufti knots and those that do. 'Tiebaff' is the name given to those where the jufti is absent, and 'Farsibaff' to those where it predominates. The terms do not appear to be used for rugs of any other centre. See Farsibaff and Khorasan.

TIFLIS (TBILISI) *Caucasian, Map: G3*
Hawley[123] refers to these rugs, but from his description they could be either Gendje or what other early writers called Tcherkess. No doubt rugs were marketed in Tiflis, and for that reason and in the absence of any more definite knowledge regarding their provenance, they were called Tiflis rugs. The use of the name as a rug description is very seldom encountered nowadays.

TIMURI (TAIMURI, TEIMURI)
This tribe, which claims descent from the Mongols, lives near the border between Afghanistan and northern Khorasan. They weave rugs which are very similar to those of the Baluchi. Bogolyubov[124] refers to rugs by the names 'Timur Afghan' and 'Timur Belouch' and provides illustrations of these in his book.

TIMURID *Persian*

Name used to describe rugs made during the reign of the Timurid dynasty (1380-1506), probably in the court manufactories of Herat. None have survived, but we know of them from their detailed depiction in miniature paintings of the period. It is interesting to note that their designs were closely related to those of the so-called 'Holbeins' of Anatolia. Towards the end of this period the scrolls and arabesques, more commonly associated with Persian carpets, began to appear. It is thought that this was a result of the influence of the arts of the book which were highly developed in Herat in the fifteenth century.

TOBREH

According to Hubel[125] this name means a 'long bag'. He does not say in which country the word is used but the name might be a different form of the word 'torba'.

TORBA *Turkoman*

Bag measuring roughly 0,8 m by 1,2 m (2ft 6in. by 4ft).

TRADE NAMES

These are as changeable as any advertising slogan but some have survived for decades. A number are mentioned as separate entries in the dictionary. A few of these do not appear at first glance to be trade names, such as the modern 'Sarouk', but there can be no doubt that names such as this are creations of commerce. A number of names are those devised by import houses for carpets made to their design specifications and over which they have the monopoly. The following is a list of a few of this type: Ajayb, made in India; Bakra, Moroccan design made in India; Bengali, Chinese design made in India; Chindia, made in India; Dildar, Chinese design made in India; Fette, Chinese rug named after the American family who owned the factory in China where they were made; Fuigi Royal, Chinese design made in Japan; Keen Lund, Chinese design made in India; Nordik and Ranji, Scandinavian designs made in India; Sirdar and Taj Mahal, made in India.

TRANSYLVANIAN *Anatolian*

Name used for a group of seventeenth and eighteenth-century rugs which were first discovered in churches in Siebenburgen (Transylvania, Romania) and were originally believed to have been made there. They were brought to the attention of the world by E. Schmutzler's publication, *Altorientalische Teppiche in Siebenburgen.* Nowadays this group of rugs is generally referred to as Transylvanian – though it is accepted that they were made in Anatolia, but precisely where is still unknown.

TSEYVA *Caucasian*

Subclassification of Kuba carpets mentioned by Hubel[126] but we suspect that his reference may have arisen from an incorrect transliteration, or even a misprint, or possibly some confusion with the 'Zejwa' referred to by Schürmann.[127] We take this view because in Hubel's list of Caucasian rugs he refers to a Zejwa but not a Tseyva whereas in his text he refers to both a Tseyva and a 'Zeyva' – but not to a Zejwa. His description of a Tseyva would appear to correspond to Schürmann's Zejwa. It is to be

133

noted that there is a rug producing village in western Turkey called Zeyve but no village or town with a name similar to Tseyva in the Caucasus.

TSHERLIK (CHERLIK) *Turkoman*
Saddle cover.

TUISSERKHAN (TUISARKAN) *Persian*
See Hamadan.

TUKASH *Turkoman*
Knotted pieces used as pan-holders; also found as 'tudadj' and 'ghazan-tutash'.

TURBELIK (TURBEHLIK)
See Mazerlik.

TURFAN FRAGMENTS
Sir Aurel Stein was born Hungarian in 1862. He became a British national in 1904, was knighted in 1912 and died in Afghanistan in 1943. During his life in the East he conducted a number of archaeological expeditions into East Turkestan, the first in 1900 and subsequent ones in 1906, 1913 and 1930. Among other valuable discoveries made during these expeditions were several fragments of knotted carpets dating from the third and sixth centuries. These are known as the Turfan Fragments, named after the city and area of Turfan where the expeditions operated. Unfortunately the fragments are too small for their design or provenance to be determined. Turfan is the Western version of Tu-lu-Fan, a city on the northern side of the Turfan Depression. It is situated in a mountain basin between the Tien Shan and Ku-lu-ko Shan-mo Mountains. An oasis city,

it has been an important trade centre for many centuries and was at one time on the northern branch of the Silk Road to Kashgar. The Depression to the south of the city is geographically a fault trough which descends to a point one hundred and fifty metres below sea level.

'TURKEY CARPETS'
As the first Oriental pile carpets to reach the West were Turkish or Anatolian, it became customary in European countries, England and the U.S.A. to speak of all Oriental carpets as 'Turkey carpets' or 'Turkish'. Turkish carpets were known in Europe from the fourteenth century but it was not until the reign of Shah Abbas (1587-1629) that Europe first saw Persian carpets. Erdmann[128] mentions an eighteenth-century reference to *tapis de Turquie persan* indicating how closely the name 'Turkey' was associated with knotted rugs. 'Turkey work' referred to both knotted and embroidered fabrics coming from the East and also to European imitations of these.

TURKIBAFF *Persian*
Name which means 'Turkish knot' usually referring to Meshed or Khorasan rugs made with the Turkish knot. See Farsibaff and Tiebaff.

TURKI SHIRAZ *Persian*
Name at one time used by Turkish and Western dealers to label some of the rugs from the Shiraz region. The probable explanation for its origin is the fact that a number of tribes living in this region, including the Qashqa'i, are Turkic in origin

134

and speak a Turkic language.

TURKISH KAZAKS *Anatolian*
Rugs from eastern Turkey that resemble
Kazaks are often given this name. These rugs
could in fact be made by any of the ethnic
groups living between the Kazak weaving
area of the Caucasus and eastern Turkey and
indeed, some are referred to as 'Kurd Kazaks'
to signify that they were made by Kurds. See
Kars, Kazak and Kurdish.

TURKOMAN *Central Asian*
According to their verbal heritage these
people are descendants of the Oghuz.
Historically the Oghuz are a Turkic people
who probably originated in the Altai
Mountain region of Central Asia which is
bounded by Mongolia, Siberia and
Khazakstan. A number of people have held
the view that this area was the birthplace of
the knotting craft, a view that acquired
considerable credence when the Pazyryk
Carpet was discovered in 1949. Not everyone
will agree with this, however, but whether
the argument will ever amount to anything
more than interesting speculation, is
impossible to say for it may be that the winds
of the steppes have long since erased the
evidence.

In historic times the Turkoman have lived
in eastern Iran, Turkmenistan which is
western Central Asia, and Afghanistan. In
spite of short-term nomadic tribal migrations
east and north, there was a gradual
movement, since at least the seventeenth
century, of the Turkoman south and west.
Towards the end of the nineteenth century
the southward flow increased as they strove
to maintain their independent way of life.

The earliest records of their complex
history first appeared in the eleventh-century
writings of Mahmud Kashghari and then in
the thirteenth-century universal history by
Rashid al-din. A more specifically Turkoman
history was written in the seventeenth
century by Abul-Ghazi Bahadur, Khan of
Khiva. After the Russian Revolution in 1917,
V.V. Barthold, the Russian historian who was
of German extraction, was officially requested
by the Turkoman and Kirghiz to write the
histories of their communities.

As far as the carpets of Central Asia are
concerned, there are brief references to them
in the writings of the early Arab historians
and of the very few travellers who penetrated
the area before the late eighteenth century.
Although it has never been clear whether
these referred to knotted or flatwoven
carpets, there can now be little doubt that the
true knotted carpet has been known and
probably made in Central Asia for at least
two thousand years. The first book on
Turkoman rugs was that of Bogolyubov[129]
published in 1908. He lived in the area as
governor of what was then known as the
Transcaspian Province of Russia. His keen
interest in and first-hand knowledge of the
area established his work as one of lasting
reference value and therefore of prime
importance in the study of Turkoman
weavings. Unfortunately the very importance
of the work has led many subsequent
students to the incorrect assumption that his
book was comprehensive and all-inclusive.

There has been a tendency in the past few
decades to try and fit all rugs which appear to
be Turkoman into one of the major groups –

Tekke, Yomut, Salor, Ersari, Saryk, Kizil Ayak, Ogurjali and Chaudor. This approach to classification, although it would certainly be true of the majority of rugs, ignores the probability of some of these rugs being the work of any of the other Turkoman tribes and also those non-Turkoman tribes which lived near them, and which are known to have woven rugs. Among these are the Ata, Arabatchi, Abdal, Goklan, Igdyr, Qarqin, Qara-dashli, Shikh, Khoja, Said and Makhtum. There is now a growing body of students who recognize the complexity and inadequacy of Turkoman rug classification and these include Thompson and Azadi. We also know of very systematic and detailed research being done in the U.S.S.R. by Elena Tsareva and others who have access not only to Bogolyubov's collection, made during the late 1800s and early 1900s, but also to the actual region, and this of course facilitates ethnographic study.

The problems of identifying Turkoman weaves arise out of many factors. Firstly, relative to the products of Turkey and Persia, our study of carpets from Central Asia is relatively recent and rudimentary. Because access to the area was extremely perilous until the late nineteenth century, Turkoman rugs were virtually unknown in the West except by hearsay. Secondly, there are no surviving examples that are contemporaneous with the earliest Turkish and Persian carpets. Thirdly, the people had no written language and coupled with this was the problem of trying to unravel the histories of people who were frequently on the move and involved in continuous internecine warfare which resulted in a rapid flux in the fortunes of many tribes. Some tribes were absorbed and assimilated by others and some vanished completely, until finally, with the advent of the Russians came a process of change which altered every aspect of Turkoman life. We have no doubt that these radical changes began with the battle of Geok Tepe in 1881, when the Tekke, who were the last tribe to hold out against the Russian advance, were decisively beaten. The next milestone in the process of change was the Bolshevik Revolution in 1917. Geok Tepe opened the area to commercial exchange and influences hitherto unknown to any significant degree. The revolution and social reorganization that followed changed the fundamentals of the Turkoman traditional way of life by severely curtailing nomadism. The influence of both these events is manifest in the products of this area. Since the First World War there has been a tremendous break with tradition in the case of all Turkoman rugs. These products are now made for sale – largely to the West – in designs that are basically Turkoman, but in colours that are not remotely traditional.

Leaving aside this modern commercial development based on synthetic dyes, and returning to the traditional Turkoman craft, the older rugs show a far greater degree of design and colour variation than those of the late nineteenth and early twentieth century. One gets the impression that tribal differences in weaving were more clearly defined the further back in history one goes. Although one cannot be certain about this it does seem likely that when the Turkoman tribes were crushed and they lost their independence the incidence of design-borrowing increased and the number of different design motifs and colours decreased and became far more stereotyped. Students of Turkoman rugs place much emphasis on the well-founded belief that conquering tribes took over and used in their own weavings the guls and ornamentation of the conquered people; but we believe that a great deal of the copying and borrowing of designs that has taken place since the third quarter of the nineteenth century has been motivated more by commerce than by tribal mores.

Individual tribes are dealt with under separate entries where some difficulties of identification are discussed.

TURSHIZ *Persian*
Former name of Kashmar, a weaving village in the Khorasan area which according to Edwards 'enjoyed the distinction of producing some of the worst carpets in all Persia'.[130] See Khorasan and Kashmar.

TUZLA *Anatolian*
Rugs from the Lake Tuzla area, north-east of Kayseri, were at one time sold under this name, but they were of little consequence and the name appears to have vanished from the sale-rooms.

UKUKI (UKUCHI) *Turkoman*
Bag used for covering the ends of the poles for the yurt (tent) while being transported, also known as 'uk bash'.

URFA *Anatolian*
Situated in south-eastern Turkey close to the Syrian border and previously known as Edessa. The city is of great historical interest and antiquity and its legendary history extends back as far as King Nimrod and the birth of Abraham. Its right to a place in the history of the knotted carpet is dubious but nevertheless dictated by what was known some decades ago as the 'Urfa Set'. The 'set' was the traditional Middle Eastern arrangement of four carpets of the same design in the main assembly room where one main carpet was flanked by two narrower ones and all three were headed by one placed transversely. But how 'Urfa Set' was imported into rug terminology is a mystery because all weaving centres of any importance would make the sets when required and Urfa was certainly not an important weaving centre. In any case its curious credentials as a rug name ensured the name's early demise.

URGÜP *Anatolian*
Province and village in central Turkey. Rugs made there in the nineteenth and twentieth centuries are known by that name. See Kayseri.

USHAK (UŞAK, OUSHAK) *Anatolian, Map, see Uşak: B3*
It is generally believed that rug making in Anatolia began with the advent of the Seljuks in the eleventh century. By the fifteenth century rugs were being produced by manufactories and independent weavers in the environs of Ushak. The origins of the Ushak rugs must therefore be looked for between these two dates. The rugs of the fifteenth, sixteenth and seventeenth centuries were widely acclaimed in Europe where they were appreciated and depicted in the

137

paintings of many artists, including Lorenzo Lotto and Hans Holbein whose names were used later to describe particular Ushak designs. The eighteenth century saw a decline in the quality of these rugs and the modern products of Ushak are vastly inferior to their illustrious ancestors. Names that have been used for various types of modern Ushaks are Enile (Inely), Yaprak, Gulistan and Kutahya.

It is interesting to note that Ushak rugs were being copied in England from the second half of the sixteenth century and a number of the later copies were at one time mistakenly attributed to the Ushak workshops.

UZBAKYA
See Afghan and Uzbek.

UZBEK (UZBEG, OZBEG) *Central Asia*
A people of Central Asia unrelated to the Turkoman. They are renowned for their textiles such as 'ikat' work and their embroideries known as 'suzanis'. No book except Bogolyubov's has shown an illustration of an Uzbek pile rug though these rugs are mentioned in the exhibition catalogue entitled 'Uzbek'.[131] We believe that there are piled rugs made by the Uzbeks but which have been wrongly attributed to the Ersari.

Vagireh (WAGIREH) *Persian*
Knotted piece woven with sections of one or more designs either as a sample for a potential purchaser or as a model for a weaver.

VERAMIN *Persian, Map: 16, Plates 77, 78*
Rugs from this town, fifty kilometres south of Tehran, do not have a long tradition. They were unknown to the early authors such as Mumford, Hawley and even Dilley, though they appear to have been made since at least the nineteenth century. According to Eiland[132] they are made by the Pazekis, a once-powerful tribe which is predominantly Kurdish. The weave structure is remote from most Kurdish work but, for that matter, so are Sennehs which are also made by Kurds.

Two distinct Veramins are marketed. Our illustration shows a manufactory one in which two wefts, one of which is dyed light blue, are used. The village rugs do not appear to have this characteristic.

VERNEH *Caucasian*
This term is very often used for a flatwoven rug, usually made of narrow strips sewn together and brocaded with a design of animals, mosques or stylized flowers. As with 'sileh' and 'djidjim' there is neither agreement as to a specific definition for 'verneh', nor is it clear how it originated.

VISS *Persian*
Hubel[133] describes rugs of this name as good commercial products from the Sultanabad area.

Waziri
These rugs are known in the trade but prior to O'Bannon no author had anything to say about them. According to O'Bannon they were woven by Ersaris in Afghanistan and apparently only during the inter-war years.

138

The name would appear to be derived from 'vizier'; to quote O'Bannon, 'These carpets take their name from the Wazirs, a Persian word meaning "minister", who ruled northern Afghanistan from the time of Abdur Rahman. To ensure control over the northern provinces where no Pushtoons lived, Abdur Rahman, who was king from 1880 to 1901, established military garrisons and permanent settlements of Pushtoon tribesmen in various provincial cities of northern Afghanistan. Shiberghan and Mazar-i-Sharif were two such principal government centres. The Governors or Wazirs of these areas forced or encouraged the Turkomans to weave carpets in these new designs, though where they got the designs from is not known. However, the Ersari Turkomans who wove them did not like the designs, and when they were no longer under pressure to make them, the production of this type of carpet ceased.'[134]

YAÇEBEDIR (YAGI-BEDIR) *Anatolian*
The dark colour of these rugs explains the name which means 'charcoal carpet'. See Bergama.

YAHYALI *Anatolian, Map, see Yahyah: D4*
Turkish rugs from the village of Yahyah in eastern Anatolia, south of Kayseri.

YAK RUGS *Chinese*
In the Western world a rug of this name signifies a coarse Chinese rug made of hair, but not necessarily yak hair.

YALAMEH *Persian*
Modern Iranian rugs from the Fars province south of Abadeh.

YAMOODI (YAMOUT)
See Afghan and Yomut.

YAPRAK *Anatolian*
See Ushak.

YAREMKENDIRLI *Anatolian*
A Kula Kendirli is a Kula with abnormally thick weft threads, three or four ply, appearing at irregular intervals. According to Hubel[135] the name 'Yaremkendirli' is used when these abnormal wefts are less thick. Both the terms are confined to the trade vernacular of local dealers because the descriptions 'thick' and 'less thick' are not defined and are therefore meaningless except as a subjective comparison.

YARKAND *East Turkestan, Map: Q5*
Town in eastern Central Asia where rugs very similar to the Kashgars and Khotans were produced and marketed. According to Schürmann, the Yarkands are structurally distinct from the other East Turkestan rugs in that 'the warp threads lie obliquely to one another, and the weft is of blue cotton'.[136]

YESILHISAR *Anatolian*
South-central Turkish rug-producing village. Its products might be sold under this name or as 'Nigde', the nearest important market town. See Nigde.

YASTIK *Anatolian*
Another form of this word is 'yestiklik' and both forms refer to small knotted pieces made for cushion covers or for sitting on. The

Persian, Turkoman and Baluchi equivalent is 'pushti'.

YATAK *Anatolian, Plates 81, 82*
Word meaning 'bed' in Turkish. Carpets so named are in fact made as sleeping mats or beds and have an exceptionally long pile. The plates illustrate a yatak made by the Yürük near Konya. See Yürük.

YEREVAN *Caucasian*
See Erivan.

YEZD (YASD) *Persian, Map: I7/J7*
Town north-west of Kerman which, according to seventeenth-century writings, was at that time as important a rug producing town as Kerman itself. No old rugs have been positively attributed to Yezd, but there is a possibility that some of the carpets, made in what Beattie[137] has called the 'vase technique', may have been made there. Similar to other Persian centres there was a hiatus between the seventeenth-century production and the late nineteenth-century revival of the craft in Yezd. Comparisons between the rugs of the two periods are obviously not possible, but modern Yezd rugs are considered to be of good quality. See Kerman.

YOLAMI *Turkoman*
Tent band, also known as 'yup' and 'bou'. See Kibitka.

YOMUT (YOMUD, YOMOUD) *Turkoman, Map: K2, J4/K4, Plates 79, 80*
Although the alternative spellings are frequently used, Barthold[138] points out that 'Yomud' is a Russian pronunciation that does not occur anywhere in Oriental sources. The correct pronunciation is 'Yomut'.

Yomut ancestry is uncertain. The tribe was not one of the original Oghuz clans listed by Mahmud Kashghari and Rashid al-din. A legend concerning its origin refers to Oghurjik, a Salor leader, who had six sons, one of the eldest being the forebear of the Yomut tribe. Whether they were formed by an offshoot of the Salor cannot be established, but they did come into existence as an identifiable group long after the Salor. Furthermore, according to Abul-Ghazi, only the Tekke and Saryk are justified in claiming a true Salor origin.

From the middle of the eighteenth century, two main groups of Yomut had become established. The southern group was located on the south-eastern shores of the Caspian Sea, on the Atrek and Gorgan Rivers. The northern group lived around Khiva on the north-western side. It is this north-western group that Abul-Ghazi included among the tribes comprising the 'Outer Salor'. The southern group had largely become settled at a relatively early stage in their history, but the northern group remained nomadic until the policy imposed after the Russian Revolution put an end to nomadism. The Turkoman nomads were notorious for brigandage and belligerence. They raided caravans and neighbouring tribes and towns to acquire the things that their unsettled way of life prevented them from producing for themselves. To fight was considered more manly than to work. The Yomut were no exception. Barthold reports an incident in the history of Khiva that was one of many that caused concern to the Khans: 'In the beginning of 1856 the Yomut carried out a successful expedition against Khiva and killed the Khan; on February 11th the vazir Muhammad Ya'quib (who was executed in the same year on the orders of the new Khan) managed to rouse the population and organise a massacre of the Yomut which lasted three and a half hours.'[139] In spite of the large number killed, the Yomut were not reduced to insignificance because after the Bolshevik Revolution their dialect became the official language of Turkmenistan.

The rugs described by dealers and many museums as 'Yomut' form a large and rather varied group which is based largely on the recurrence of certain design motifs. We are doubtful that all these rugs are Yomut work, and for this reason have devised the term 'greater Yomut group'. We also use the term to describe the tribes which were associated with the Yomut, such as the Ogurjalis, Igdyr, Abdal, Ata, Arabatchi, Goklan, and Khoja. This association was determined by geographic proximity; it may have included subjection or assimilation of weaker tribes, but was not necessarily a genealogical relationship. The suggestion we are making is that several, if not all of these tribes made some of the rugs which are commonly called 'Yomut', and we base this suggestion on the following points: firstly, all these tribes are believed to have made knotted rugs, but we do not know which rugs, with the possible exception of the Ogurjalis; secondly, Bogolyubov's[140] book shows an illustration of an engsi (door-hanging) which he says is the work of the Igdyr tribe of the Yomut. Most modern dealers take no notice of this rather important piece of evidence and would

simply call such a rug 'Yomut'; the third point is that among the rugs attributed to the Yomut are a number which undoubtedly have some Yomut characteristics but nevertheless show sufficient differences in design, colour and structure to indicate that a different attribution must at least be considered. We refer in this regard to Azadi's Plate 10 to which he gives the tentative attribution of 'Arabatchi, Igdyr, Abdal . . .'[141]

Another factor which has a bearing on the situation is that two distinct Yomut weaves are identifiable. Our Plate 79 shows the weave pattern of an old engsi where the knots all lie on an even plane. The other weave more commonly associated with Yomut work has a ridged appearance along the line of the warps. Plate 80 is included because the rug would generally be described as a Yomut, but it may yet prove to be wrongly attributed, and to have been made by some other group such as the Ata or the Ogurjalis. Whether these two weaves can be associated with the northern and southern sections of the Yomut tribe is not yet known, and it may even be found that more weave subgroups will emerge under further systematic study.

Some authorities make positive attributions to the Ogurjalis people, others disregard them as a distinct weaving group. The former draw attention to the use of colour in some of the Yomut rugs which they say is indicative of a Caucasian influence. It is true that at the beginning of the nineteenth century the Ogurjalis inhabited the area north of the Atrek and Gurgan Rivers on the shores of the Caspian Sea. It is also probable that there was indeed a Caucasian influence on the Turkoman products in that area but in

141

our opinion there is insufficient evidence to attribute all the rugs of that genre to a particular tribe.

YÜN YÜRÜK
We suspect that this is one of those in-group Istanbul dealer terms, used to differentiate between rugs with wool and those with goat-hair warp threads. 'Yün' means 'wool', but all Yürük rugs are wool apart from a variable use of goat-hair in the warp yarn.

YUNTDAG *Anatolian*
Village between Bergama and Izmir in western Anatolia. Rugs and kelims made there in the nineteenth and twentieth centuries are sold under this name.

YUP
Tent band, also known as 'bou' and 'yolami'. See Kibitka.

YÜRÜK *Anatolian, Plates 81, 82*
Turkish word meaning 'nomad'. In rug nomenclature the word was originally applied to nomadic rugs from the Karaman province and eastern Anatolia. Nowadays the application is much wider; it is used to describe any rug other than a manufactory piece which cannot be more accurately described. One finds, for example, the name 'Konya Yürük', and this is intended to mean a tribal or nomadic piece with a Konya design influence, but not made in a manufactory. The weave pattern of Yürüks show a wide diversity and this is explained by the fact that the Yürüks are strongly influenced by the town and village weavings of the area where they live or spend most of their time. Some rugs which have been described as Yürüks are without doubt Kurdish work and would be more appropriately called Kurdish. Plates 81 and 82 illustrate a 'yatak' – Turkish for 'bed' – from the Konya area. See Sultan and Kurdish.

ZABOL *Persian, Map: L8*
See Sistan.

ZAHIR SHAHI
See Afghan.

ZARA *Anatolian*
Rug weaving village in central Anatolia. Rugs produced there in the nineteenth and twentieth centuries are sold under this name or as Malatya.

ZARAND *Persian, Map: J8*
Town north of Kerman that has lent its name to a rug size, 138 cm by 69 cm (4 ft 6 in. by 2 ft 3 in.)

ZARCHARAK (ZAROCHEREK) *Persian*
Dimensional term for a rug about 122 cm by 81 cm (4ft by 2ft 8in.)

ZARIF *Anatolian*
Trade name for a modern Turkish rug, mentioned only by Dilley[142] who says that it is a contraction of 'Zarifali' meaning 'refinement'.

ZAROCHEREK *Persian*
See Zarcharak.

ZARONIM *Persian*

Dimensional term for a rug 152 cm by 100 cm (5 ft by 3 ft 3 in.)

ZEJWA *Caucasian, Map: H3*
See Daghestan and Kuba.

ZEL-I-SULTAN *Persian, Plates 83, 84*
A number of authorities refer only to a design by this name. Others have recognized that a structurally distinctive type of rug of this name was made. Their manufacture could not have lasted longer than a few decades in the late nineteenth or early twentieth century. Dilley[143] said that there was an obvious relationship between old Sarouks, Feraghans, 'Zelli Sultans' and Mushkabads. The rug shown in Plates 83 and 84 obviously belongs to a separate class for although it is somewhat similar in structure to the old Sarouks (Plates 63 and 64), it is nevertheless distinctive, and is also different from the old Feraghan (Plates 19 and 20). It is not possible at this stage to say where they were made but the Sarouk-Feraghan area appears to be the most likely locality.

ZENJAN (ZANJAN, SENDSHAN, TSANYAN) *Persian, Map, see Zanjan: H5*
These rugs are made in a group of villages south-east of Mianeh. They acquired their name from the principal marketing village, but were once included in the Hamadan group as they were sold there. Low grade examples were known as 'Zenjan Mosuls'. Some authorities consider them to be made by Kurds.

ZEYVE *Anatolian*
A co-operative at this town in western Turkey produces Isparta-type rugs. Most Zeyve rugs are sold as Çal.

ZHUPAR *Persian*
Kerman village rug of a distinctive design.

ZIEGLER *Persian*
In the latter part of the nineteenth century Ziegler and Company of Manchester, England, started manufactories in Tabriz and Sultanabad. These rugs were sold as 'Ziegler rugs'. See Sultanabad.

ZILE *Anatolian and Caucasian*
The name has two uses. Zile is a rug weaving village near Yahyah in north-eastern Turkey. Some of the rugs made there have been sold as Yahyali. The second use of the name is as an alternate spelling for Sileh. See Sileh.

References

1 Hartley Clark, *Bokhara, Turkoman and Afghan Rugs* (London, 1922), pp. 104-106.

2 Arthur U. Dilley, *Oriental Rugs and Carpets* (Philadelphia, 1959), p. 195.

3 George W. O'Bannon, *The Turkoman Carpet* (London, 1974), pp. 90-153.

4 Mahmud Kashghari was a Turkish writer of the eleventh century who lived in Baghdad. He compiled, possibly during the years 1071 to 1074, a very comprehensive Turko-Arabic dictionary for use by Arabs. It contained fragments of the once richly developed lyric and epic literature of the Central Asian Turks. Rashid al-din (1247-1318) was a Persian statesman and author of a universal history. He was historian to the Mongol ruler of Persia, Gazan (1294-1304). Both of these writers compiled lists of the Turkoman tribes and these have been an important part of the source material used in all studies of the Turkoman people. In this work, these two writers are quoted always according to V.V. Barthold, *Four Studies on the History of Central Asia* (Leiden, 1962).

5 A. Cecil Edwards, *The Persian Carpet* (London, 1975), pp. 277-280.

6 Ulrich Schürmann, *Caucasian Rugs* (Braunschweig, 1965), p. 80.

7 Reinhard G. Hubel, *The Book of Carpets* (London, 1971), p. 283.

8 O'Bannon, *Turkoman Carpet*, p. 127.

9 Murray L. Eiland, *Oriental Rugs* (Greenwich, 1973), p. 158.

10 F.R. Martin, *A History of Oriental Carpets Before 1800* (Vienna, 1908), p. 91, Fig. 214.

11 Edwards, *Persian Carpet*, p. 310.

12 Nora Kubie, *The Road to Nineveh* (London, 1963), pp. 100, 103.

13 Schürmann, *Caucasian Rugs*, pp. 83-91.

14 O'Bannon, *Turkoman Carpet*, pp. 58-59.

15 Heinrich Jacoby, *How to Know Oriental Carpets and Rugs* (London, 1967), p. 30.

16 Noel Hobbs, 'Baluchi Weavings: a Collector's Study and Evaluation', in David Black and Clive Loveless, comps, *Rugs of the Wandering Baluchi* (London, 1976), p. 16.

17 Dilley, *Oriental Rugs* p. 133.

18 John Kimberly Mumford, *Oriental Rugs* (London, 1915), pp. 189-191.

19 Hubel, *Book of Carpets*, p. 133.
20 Ibid., p. 50.
21 Ibid., p. 86.
22 Mumford, *Oriental Rugs*, p. 143.
23 Kurt Erdmann, *Oriental Carpets* (London, 1962), pp. 27-29.
24 Maurice S. Dimand and Jean Mailey, *Oriental Rugs in the Metropolitan Museum of Art* (New York, 1973), pp. 194-200.
25 Friedrich Sarre, 'Die Ägyptische Herkunft der Sogen. Damaskus Teppiche', *Zeitschrift für Bildende Kunst* 32, 1921, pp. 75-82.
26 Jacoby, *How to Know Oriental Carpets*, p. 41.
27 O'Bannon, *Turkoman Carpet*, pp. 129-130.
28 A.A. Bogolyubov, *Carpets of Central Asia* (Ramsdell, 1973), Plates 7, 8.
29 Ulrich Schürmann, *Central-Asian Rugs* (Frankfurt-on-Main, 1969), Plates 6, 7.
30 Christopher Dunham Reed, intro., *Turkoman Rugs* (Cambridge, 1966), Illus. 2.
31 Schürmann, *Central-Asian Rugs*, Plate 26.
32 H.A. Lorenz, *A View of Chinese Rugs* (London & Boston, 1972), p. 76.
33 D.H.G. Wegner, 'Nomad and Peasant Rugs in Afghanistan', *Baessler Archives* New Ed. 12, 1964, p. 146.
34 O'Bannon, *Turkoman Carpet*, Illus. p. 2.
35 Schürmann, *Central-Asian Rugs*, Plate 60.
36 Schürmann, *Caucasian Rugs*, p. 31.
37 Ibid., pp. 252-347.
38 Wilhelm von Bode and Ernst Kühnel, *Antique Rugs from the Near East* (London, 1970), p. 75.
39 Kurt Erdmann, *Seven Hundred Years of Oriental Carpets* (London, 1970), p. 37.
40 Hubel, *Book of Carpets*, p. 93.
41 Walter A. Hawley, *Oriental Rugs; Antique and Modern* (New York, 1970), p. 205.
42 Schürmann, *Caucasian Rugs*, p. 49.
43 Anthony N. Landreau and W.R. Pickering, *From the Bosporus to Samarkand; Flat-Woven Rugs* (Washington, 1969), p. 14.
44 Hubel, *Book of Carpets*, p. 50.
45 Dimand and Mailey, *Oriental Rugs*, pp. 263-267.
46 Charles Grant Ellis, *Early Caucasian Rugs* (Washington, 1975).
47 Kudret H. Turkhan, *Islamic Rugs* (London, 1968), p. 93.
48 Jacoby, *How to Know Oriental Carpets*, p. 58.
49 Albrecht Hopf, *Oriental Carpets and Rugs* (London, 1962), p. 67.
50 Mumford, *Oriental Rugs*, pp. 129, 131.
51 Hawley, *Oriental Rugs*, pp. 224-225.
52 Schürmann, *Caucasian Rugs*, pp. 144-162.
53 Bogolyubov, *Carpets of Central Asia*, Plate 22.
54 Hawley, *Oriental Rugs*, p. 156.
55 Hubel, *Book of Carpets*, p. 196.
56 Nicolas Fokker, *Persian and Other Oriental Carpets for Today* (London, 1973), pp. 70, 71.
57 Dimand and Mailey, *Oriental Rugs*, pp. 34, 38.
58 Mumford, *Oriental Rugs*, p. 151.
59 Hopf, *Oriental Carpets and Rugs*, p. 106.
60 Bogolyubov, *Carpets of Central Asia*, Plate 16.
61 Jacoby, *How to Know Oriental Carpets*, p. 71.
62 Schürmann, *Caucasian Rugs*, pp. 28-42.
63 Dilley, *Oriental Rugs*, p. 277.
64 Edwards, *Persian Carpet*, p. 62.
65 Bogolyubov, *Carpets of Central Asia*, Plates 29, 30.
66 Schürmann, *Central-Asian Rugs*, pp. 35, 116.
67 Eliza Dunn, *Rugs in their Native Land*

(New York, 1920), pp. 88-89.

68 Edwards, *Persian Carpet*, p. 334.

69 Schürmann, *Caucasian Rugs*, pp. 56-109.

70 Ibid., p. 14.

71 George Vernadsky, *A History of Russia. Vol. 3: Russia at the Dawn of the Modern Age* (New Haven & London, 1959), p. 249.

72 Mumford, *Oriental Rugs*, p. 123.

73 O'Bannon, *Turkoman Carpet*, p. 59.

74 Werner Grote-Hasenbalg, *Masterpieces of Oriental Rugs* (Berlin, 1922), Vol. 3, Plates 105, 106.

75 Schürmann, *Central-Asian Rugs*, p. 36.

76 Bogolyubov, *Carpets of Central Asia*, Plates 31, 32, 53-56.

77 Barthold, *Four Studies*, Vol. 3, p. 151.

78 Wegner, 'Nomad and Peasant Rugs in Afghanistan', p. 145.

79 Bogolyubov, *Carpets of Central Asia*, Plate 4.

80 Mumford, *Oriental Rugs*, p. 192.

81 Jacoby, *How to Know Oriental Carpets*, p. 85.

82 Hubel, *Book of Carpets*, p. 184.

83 J. Iten-Maritz, *Le Tapis Turc* (Fribourg, 1976), p. 80.

84 Mumford, *Oriental Rugs*, p. 131.

85 Erdmann, *Seven Hundred Years*, p. 60.

86 Siawosch Azadi, *Turkoman Carpets* (Fishguard, 1975), p. 18.

87 Edwards, *Persian Carpet*, p. 139.

88 Jacoby, *How to Know Oriental Carpets*, pp. 92-93.

89 Mumford, *Oriental Rugs*, pp. 115, 243.

90 Jacoby, *How to Know Oriental Carpets*, pp. 94-95.

91 Hubel, *Book of Carpets*, p. 50.

92 Lorenz, *View of Chinese Rugs*, p. 152.

93 J.M.A. Thompson, ed., 'Editor's Introduction to the Plates', in A.A. Bogolyubov, *Carpets of Central Asia*, opposite Plate 19.

94 Geoffrey Lewis, *Modern Turkey* (London, 1974), p. 30.

95 Landreau and Pickering, *Bosporus to Samarkand*, p. 14.

96 Hubel, *Book of Carpets*, p. 70.

97 O'Bannon, *Turkoman Carpet*, p. 60.

98 S.I. Rudenko, *The World's Most Ancient Carpets and Fabrics* (Moscow, 1968).

99 Nejat Diyarbekerli, 'New Light on the Pazyryk Carpet'. Paper read at the International Conference on Oriental Carpets, London, 1976.

100 Erdmann, *Seven Hundred Years*, p. 75.

101 Sylvia Matheson, *The Tigers of Baluchistan* (London, 1967), p. 23.

102 J.A. Boyle in exhibition catalogue, 'The Qashqa'i of Iran' (Manchester, 1976), p. 8.

103 Pierre Oberling, *The Qashqa'i Nomads of Fars* (The Hague, 1974), p. 31.

104 Martin, *History of Oriental Carpets*, Fig. 161.

105 Clark, *Bokhara, Turkoman and Afghan Rugs*, p. 106.

106 Dilley, *Oriental Rugs*, p. 200.

107 Bogolyubov, *Carpets of Central Asia*, p. 19.

108 Oktay Aslanapa, *Turkish Arts* (Istanbul, 1961), p. 14.

109 Mumford, *Oriental Rugs*, p. 198.

110 Ibid., p. 197.

111 Hawley, *Oriental Rugs*, p. 130.

112 Dilley, *Oriental Rugs*, p. 125.

113 Edwards, *Persian Carpet*, pp. 144-145.

114 Eiland, *Oriental Rugs*, p. 60.

115 A.F. Kendrick and C.E.C. Tattersall, *Hand-Woven Carpets, Oriental & European* (New York, 1973), p. 175.

116 Dilley, *Oriental Rugs*, p. 106.

117 Carl Hopf, *Old Persian Carpets and their Artistic Values* (Munich, 1913), p. 25.

118 Schürmann, *Caucasian Rugs*, pp. 62-81.

119 Edwards, *Persian Carpet*, p. 187.

120 Schürmann, *Caucasian Rugs*, pp. 53-57.

121 Barthold, *Four Studies*, Vol. 3, p. 133.

122 Philip Denwood, *The Tibetan Carpet* (Warminster, 1974), p. 2.

123 Hawley, *Oriental Rugs*, p. 219.

124 Bogolyubov, *Carpets of Central Asia*, Plates 35, 48.

125 Hubel, *Book of Carpets*, p. 50.

126 Ibid., p. 133.

127 Schürmann, *Caucasian Rugs*, p. 112.

128 Erdmann, *Seven Hundred Years*, p. 23.

129 Bogolyubov, *Carpets of Central Asia*.

130 Edwards, *Persian Carpet*, p. 173.

131 David Lindahl and Thomas Knorr, in exhibition catalogue, 'Uzbek' (Basle, 1975); Bogolyubov, *Carpets of Central Asia*, Plate 33.

132 Eiland, *Oriental Rugs*, p. 69.

133 Hubel, *Book of Carpets*, p. 193.

134 O'Bannon, *Turkoman Carpet*, p. 145.

135 Hubel, *Book of Carpets*, p. 80.

136 Schürmann, *Central-Asian Rugs*, p. 155.

137 May H. Beattie, in exhibition catalogue, 'Carpets of Central Persia' (England, 1976), pp. 7-13.

138 Barthold, *Four Studies*, Vol. 3, p. 132, n. 1.

139 Ibid., p. 167.

140 Bogolyubov, *Carpets of Central Asia*, Plate 16.

141 Azadi, *Turkoman Carpets*, Plate 10.

142 Dilley, *Oriental Rugs*, p. 277.

143 Ibid., p. 124.

Bibliography

Allen, W.E.D., *A History of the Georgian People*. London: Kegan, Paul, Trench, Trübner, 1932.

Arberry, A.J., ed., *The Legacy of Persia*. Oxford: Clarendon Press, 1953; repr. 1968.

Aslanapa, Oktay, *Turkish Arts*. Istanbul: Dogan Kardes, 1961.

Azadi, Siawosch, *Turkoman Carpets*, translated by Robert Pinner. Hamburg: n.p., 1970; rev. and repr. Fishguard, Wales: Crosby Press, 1975.

Barthold, V.V., *Four Studies on the History of Central Asia*, 3 vols; translated by V. and T. Minorsky. Leiden: Brill, 1956; repr. 1962.

Beaumont, Roberts, *Woollen and Worsted*. London: G. Bell, 1919.

Bennett, Ian, *Book of Oriental Carpets and Rugs*. London: Hamlyn, 1972.

Black, David and Loveless, Clive, comps, *Rugs of the Wandering Baluchi*. London: David Black Oriental Carpets, 1976.

Blanch, Lesley, *The Sabres of Paradise*. London: John Murray, 1960.

Bogolyubov, Andrei Andreyevich, *Carpets of Central Asia*, 2 pts. St Petersburg: State Printing Office, 1908-1909; rev. ed. edited by J.M.A. Thompson. Ramsdell, England: Crosby Press, 1973.

Brockelmann, Carl, *History of the Islamic Peoples*. Munich: Oldenbourg, 1939; translated by J. Carmichael and M. Perlmann. London: Routledge & Kegan Paul, 1949; repr. 1964.

Catalogue of Iran Carpet Company: *Persian Carpet Appreciation*, March 1973.

Catalogues to Exhibitions:

'Afghan Handwoven Carpets'. Kabul: n.p., 1975.

'The Arts of Islam'. England: The Arts Council of Great Britain, 1976.

'Carpets of Central Persia', text by May H. Beattie. England: World of Islam Festival Publishing, 1976.

'Lion Rugs from Fars', text by Parviz Tanavoli. Oshkosh, Wisc.: printed by Castle-Pierce, 1974.

'Prayer Rugs', text by Richard Ettinghausen, Maurice S. Dimand, Louise W. Mackie and Charles Grant Ellis. Washington, D.C.: Textile Museum, 1974.

'The Qashqā'i of Iran', introduced by J.A. Boyle. Manchester: Whitworth Art Gallery, 1976.

'The Splendour of Turkish Weaving', by Louise W. Mackie. Washington, D.C.: Textile Museum, 1973.

'Textilkunst der Steppen- und Bergvölker Zentralasiens', introduced by Dietrich H.G. Wegner. Basle: Gewerbemuseum, 1974.

'Tribal Animal Covers from Iran', text by Amedeo de Franchis and Jenny Housego. Tehran: Tehran Rug Society, 1975.

'Turkoman Weaving Including Beluch', text by Raymond Benardout. London: printed by Lund Humphries, 1974.

'Uzbek', introduced by David Lindahl and Thomas Knorr. Basle: printed by Zbinden Druck, 1975.

Clark, Hartley, *Bokhara, Turkoman and Afghan Rugs.* London: John Lane The Bodley Head, 1922.

De Calatchi, Robert, *Oriental Carpets,* 2 ed. Rutland, Vermont & Tokyo: Charles E. Tuttle, 1970.

Denwood, Philip, *The Tibetan Carpet.* Warminister, England: Aris and Phillips, 1974.

Dilley, Arthur U., *Oriental Rugs and Carpets,* revised by Maurice S. Dimand. Philadelphia: Lippincott, 1959.

Dimand, Maurice S. and Mailey, Jean, *Oriental Rugs in the Metropolitan Museum of Art.* New York: Metropolitan Museum of Art, 1973.

Diyarbekerli, Nejat, 'New Light on the Pazyryk Carpet'. Paper read at the International Conference on Oriental Carpets, London, 1976.

Dunn, Eliza, *Rugs in their Native Land.* New York: Dodd, Mead, 1920.

Edwards, A. Cecil, *The Persian Carpet.* London: Duckworth, 1953; repr. 1975.

Eiland, Murray L., *Oriental Rugs; A Comprehensive Guide.* Greenwich, Conn.: New York Graphic Society, 1973.

Ellis, Charles Grant, *Early Caucasian Rugs.* Washington, D.C.: Textile Museum, 1976.

Emery, Irene, *The Primary Structures of Fabrics.* Washington, D.C.: Textile Museum, 1966.

Encyclopaedia Britannica, 15 ed., 1974.

Encyclopaedia of Islam, 5 vols. Leiden: Brill; London: Luzac, 1913-1938.

Erdmann, Kurt, *Oriental Carpets,* translated by Charles Grant Ellis. London: Zwemmer, [preface] 1962.

Erdmann, Kurt, *Seven Hundred Years of Oriental Carpets.* Germany: Bussesche, 1966; translated by M.H. Beattie and H. Herzog. London: Faber, 1970.

Fokker, Nicolas, *Persian and Other Oriental Carpets for Today.* London: George Allen & Unwin, 1973.

Formenton, Fabio, *Oriental Rugs and Carpets,* translated by Pauline L. Phillips. London: Hamlyn, 1972.

Gans-Ruedin, E., *Antique Oriental Carpets.* London: Thames and Hudson, 1975.

Gans-Ruedin, E., *Modern Oriental Carpets; From the Seventeenth to the Early Twentieth Century,* translated by R. and E. Bartlett. London: Thames and Hudson, 1975.

Grote-Hasenbalg, Werner, *Masterpieces of Oriental Rugs,* 3 vols; translated by G. Barry Gifford. Berlin: Scarabaeus, [introduction] 1922.

Hawley, Walter A., *Oriental Rugs; Antique and Modern.* New York: John Lane, 1913; repr. New York: Dover Publications, 1970.

Hopf, Albrecht, *Oriental Carpets and Rugs.* Tübingen: Ernst Wasmuth, 1961; translated by D. Woodward, London: Thames and Hudson, 1962.

Hopf, Carl, *Old Persian Carpets and their Artistic Values,* 2 ed. Munich: n.p., 1913.

Hubel, Reinhard G., *The Book of Carpets.* Berlin: Ullstein, 1964; translated by Katherine Watson, London: Barrie & Jenkins, 1971.

Iten-Maritz, J., *Le Tapis Turc.* Fribourg: Office du Livre, 1976.

Jacobsen, Charles W., *Oriental Rugs; A Complete Guide.* Rutland, Vermont and Tokyo: Charles E. Tuttle, 1962.

Jacoby, Heinrich, *How to Know Oriental Carpets and Rugs,* 2 ed. London: George Allen & Unwin, 1962; repr. 1967.

Jettmar, Karl, *The Art of the Steppes.* London: Methuen, 1964.

Kendrick, A.F. and Tattersall, C.E.C., *Handwoven Carpets, Oriental & European.* London: Benn Brothers, 1922; repr. New York: Dover Publications, 1973.

Kubie, Norah, *The Road to Nineveh.* London: Cassell, 1963.

Kühnel, Ernst, *Islamic Art and Architecture.* Stuttgart: Kröner, 1962; translated by Katherine Watson, London: G. Bell, 1966.

Landreau, Anthony N. and Pickering, W.R., *From the Bosporus to Samarkand; Flat-woven Rugs.* Washington, D.C.: Textile Museum, 1969.

Lang, David M., *The Georgians.* London: Thames and Hudson, 1966.

Lang, David M., *Modern History of Georgia.* London: Weidenfeld & Nicolson, 1962.

Lewis, Geoffrey, *Modern Turkey.* London: Ernest Benn, 1974.

Lewis, G. Griffin, *The Practical Book of Oriental Rugs.* Philadelphia: Lippincott, 1911; 5 ed., 1920.

Lorenz, H.A., *A View of Chinese Rugs from the Seventeenth to the Twentienth Century.* London and Boston: Routledge & Kegan Paul, 1972.

Martin, F.R., *A History of Oriental Carpets Before 1800.* Vienna: State and Court Printing Office, 1908.

Matheson, Sylvia, *The Tigers of Baluchistan.* London: Arthur Barker, 1967.

McMullan, Joseph V., *Islamic Carpets.* New York: Near Eastern Art Research Center, 1965.

McMullan, Joseph V. and Reichert, Donald O., *The George Walter Vincent and Belle Townsley Smith Collection of Islamic Rugs.* Springfield, Mass.: George Walter Vincent Smith Art Museum, n.d.

Milhofer, S.A., *Die Teppiche Zentralasiens.* Hanover: Fackelträger, 1968.

Morier, James, *The Adventures of Hajji Baba of Ispahan,* 2 ed. n.p., 1824[?]; repr. London: Harrap, 1948.

Mumford, John Kimberly, *Oriental Rugs.* New York: Charles Scribner's Sons, 1900; 4 ed., London: Sampson Low, Marston, [preface] 1915.

O'Bannon, George W., *The Turkoman Carpet.* London: Duckworth, 1974.

Oberling, Pierre, *The Qashqa'i Nomads of Fars.* The Hague: Mouton, 1974.

O'Donovan, E., *The Merv Oasis.* London: Smith, Elder, 1882.

Reed, Christopher Dunham, intro., *Turkoman Rugs.* Cambridge, Mass.: Fogg Art Museum, 1966.

Rudenko, S.I., *The World's Most Ancient Carpets and Fabrics.* Moscow: n.p., 1968.

Sarre, Friedrich, 'Die Ägyptische Herkunft der Sogen. Damaskus Teppiche', *Zeitschrift für Bildende Kunst* 32, 1921.

Schürmann, Ulrich, *Caucasian Rugs.* Braunschweig: Klinkhardt & Biermann, 1965; translated by A. Grainge, London: George Allen & Unwin, n.d.

Schürmann, Ulrich, *Central-Asian Rugs,* translated by A. Grainge. Frankfurt-on-Main: Osterrieth, 1969.

Scobey, Joan, *Rugs & Wall Hangings.* New York: Dial Press, 1974.

Skrine, F.H. and Ross, E.D., *The Heart of Asia.* London: Methuen, 1899.

Stevens, Sir Roger, *The Land of the Great Sophy.*

London: Methuen, 1962.

Sümerbank, *Samples of the Old Turkish Carpets and Kilims.* Istanbul: Sümerbank, 1961.

Sumner, B.H. *Survey of Russian History.* London: Duckworth, 1944.

Tattersall, C.E.C., *Notes on Carpet Knotting and Weaving.* London: Victoria and Albert Museum, 1920; repr. 1969.

Thompson, J.M.A., ed., 'Editor's Introduction to the Plates', in A.A. Bogolyubov, *Carpets of Central Asia,* 2 pts; rev. ed. Ramsdell, England: Crosby Press, 1973.

Tschebull, Raoul, *Kazak Carpets of the Caucasus.* New York: Near Eastern Art Research Center, 1971.

Turkhan, Kudret H., *Islamic Rugs.* London: Arthur Barker, 1968.

Vernadsky, George, *A History of Russia.* Vol. 3: *The Mongols and Russia.* Vol. 4: *Russia at the Dawn of the Modern Age.* New Haven & London: Yale University Press, 1953, 1959.

Von Bode, Wilhelm and Kühnel, Ernst, *Antique Rugs from the Near East,* 4 ed. rev. Germany: n.p., 1902; translated by C.G. Ellis, London: G. Bell, 1970.

Von Haxthausen, Baron, *The Tribes of the Caucasus.* London: n.p., 1835.

Wagner, M., *Travels in Persia, Georgia and Kurdistan,* 3 vols. London: n.p., 1856.

Wardrop, Sir Oliver, *The Kingdom of Georgia.* London: Sampson, Low, 1888.

Wegner, D.H.G., 'Nomad and Peasant Rugs in Afghanistan', *Baessler Archives* New Ed. 12, 1964.

Wheeler, Geoffrey, *The Modern History of Soviet Central Asia.* New York: Praeger, 1964.

Williams, Gwyn, *Eastern Turkey: A Guide and History.* London: Faber, 1972.

Wolff, Joseph, *Narrative of a Mission to Bokhara,* abr. ed., edited by G. Wint. London: Routledge & Kegan Paul, 1969.

Colour plates

Akstafa

1,88m by 1,37m (6ft 2in. by 4ft 6in.) second half nineteenth century

PLATE 1

The appearance of the weft has nothing in common with the rugs of the Kazak group although geographically the Akstafas were closer to the Kazak area than to the Shirvan area. They are in fact structurally related to the rugs of the Shirvan group and the ripple appearance of the weft is common to all rugs from the eastern Caucasus. There are variations in the Akstafa weave patterns but we have not found an Akstafa design made in the Kazak technique.

PLATE 2

Baku

1,91m by 1,14m (6ft 3in. by 3ft 9in.) second half nineteenth century

PLATE 3

The ripple appearance of the weft, the shape of the asymmetrical knots and the slight depression of alternate warps are features found in common with most groups of rugs from the eastern Caucasus. The Baku rugs are allegedly distinguishable by design and colour – a statement dealt with in the text. They are not distinguishable on a structural basis.

PLATE 4

157

Belouch

3,23m by 1,55m (10ft 7in. by 5ft 1in.) second half nineteenth century

PLATE 5

The knot is asymmetrical. Two weft shoots of undyed brown wool are used after every row of knots. The weft lines are visible along their complete traverse, and the combination of this feature with the shape of the nodes is distinctive of the Belouch weave pattern. A degree of depression of alternate warps is found, though that is not a common feature.

PLATE 6

159

Bijar

2,08m by 1,52m (6ft 10in. by 5ft) second half nineteenth
century

PLATE 7

The warp lines are imperceptible. Alternate warps are depressed to the degree that one of the two nodes comprising each
knot is completely hidden behind its partner. Some of the weft
lines are partially visible but where they are, they do not appear
as straight lines across the rug. The colour of the weft is not a
distinguishing feature as various colours are used and sometimes more than one colour in the same rug. The shape of the
knots is distinctive.

160

PLATE 8

161

Chaudor

1,47m by 1,27m (4ft 10in. by 4ft 2in.) early nineteenth century

PLATE 9

A degree of depression of alternate warps is a common feature but the appearance of the weft and the node shape are the features which set the Chaudor weave pattern apart from all other Turkoman rugs. There is no possibility of confusing it with the weave pattern of the Yomut tribes of which the Chaudors were at one stage believed to be an offshoot.

PLATE 10

163

Chi Chi

1,73m by 1,25m (5ft 8in. by 4ft 1in.) mid nineteenth century

PLATE 11

A ripple appearance of the weft is common to the majority of the rugs of the eastern Caucasus, but that feature is displayed in this rug to a degree which is unusual even within the Chi Chi group. In refinement of technique the weave pattern of this rug is also exceptional.

PLATE 12

Daghestan

1,52m by 0,91m (5ft by 3ft) nineteenth century

PLATE 13

Where sufficient of the weft traverse is visible, it has a ripple appearance, a feature exemplified to an extreme degree by the Chi Chi (Plate 11). There is no feature of this weave pattern which is exclusive to the Daghestan area. This point is more fully discussed in the dictionary and the monograph.

166

PLATE 14

167

Ersari Afghan

2,79m by 2,16m (9ft 2in. by 7ft 1in.) mid nineteenth century

PLATE 15

The use of an undyed weft which is visible along its entire length is a characteristic feature. On the vertical line, the nodes of the asymmetrical knots are longer than they are wide. A degree of depression of alternate warps appears to be a development of more recent times. The Ersari Afghan weave pattern has an overall coarser and more fibrous appearance than the weave patterns of other Turkoman rugs.

168

PLATE 16

169

Ersari Beshir

2,21m by 1,12m (7ft 3in. by 3ft 8in.) mid nineteenth century

PLATE 17

This weave pattern displays the same features as the Ersari Afghan (Plate 15) indicating the work of the same tribe but from different areas. Other rugs of the Ersari Beshir, possibly those made near Bokhara and correspondingly further from the Afghanistan highlands, show a far more refined version of the same weave pattern.

PLATE 18

171

Feraghan

2,88m by 1,55m (9ft 5in. by 5ft 1in.) second half nineteenth century

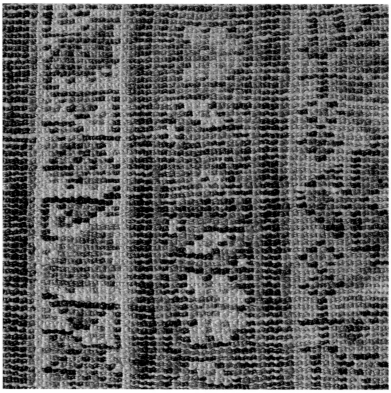

PLATE 19

Although the ripple appearance of the weft is common to a number of weave patterns, the shape of the nodes and the juxtaposition of the nodes of each knot make the Feraghan weave pattern distinguishable. Each of the north-west Persian groups of rugs, which include the Sarouk, Senneh, Feraghan, Bijar and Hamadan, has a weave pattern which is readily distinguishable from the others – a remarkable fact when one considers the proximity of the weavers.

172

PLATE 20

173

Ghiordes

2,39m by 1,65m (7ft 10in. by 5ft 5in.) early nineteenth century

PLATE 21

This is not a very fine version of the old Ghiordes weave pattern but the detail is sufficient to enable one to distinguish it from the Panderma copies of the old Ghiordes designs. The depression of alternate warps is invariable, and this, in conjunction with the node shapes, is the feature which distinguishes these rugs on a structural basis from others such as the Kula (Plate 45) and the Ladik (Plate 47).

PLATE 22

175

Hamadan

1,98m by 1,25m (6ft 6in. by 4ft 1in.) nineteenth century

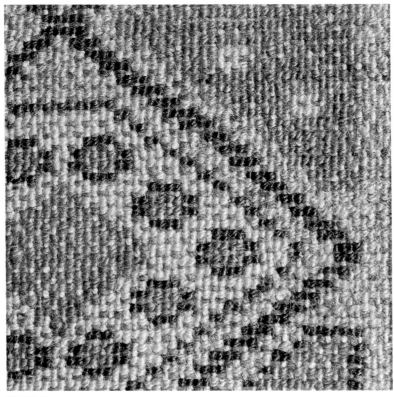

PLATE 23

The single weft passes over and under alternate warps; where it passes under, the warp thread is exposed. The next weft shoot passes over the warp which the preceding shoot passed under, and this procedure produces on every three lines of weft, the characteristic quincunx appearance of the exposed warps, like the pattern of a 'five' on a dice. Compare this weave pattern with another very different single-wefted weave, the Senneh (Plate 69).

176

PLATE 24

177

Heriz

1,78m by 1,78m (5ft 10in. by 5ft 10in.) second half nineteenth century

PLATE 25

Only one of the two nodes comprising each knot is visible, but unlike the Kerman (Plate 35) the visible node is not always contiguous with the visible node of the next knot in the row. The weft line is irregular both with regard to thickness and visibility. It frequently appears to fill the gap between the visible nodes, lending a 'string-of-beads' appearance to the weft line. The weave pattern of this beautiful rug is a very refined and compact version of the Heriz type.

PLATE 26

Isfahan

1,98m by 1,35m (6ft 6in. by 4ft 5in.) nineteenth century

PLATE 27

The weft appears in streaks of irregular thickness but it is not visible along its complete traverse as in the old Sarouks (Plate 63). This feature is the main characteristic of the Isfahan weave pattern and is to be seen in some of the early so-called 'Indo-Isfahans', a fact which indicates to us that they were made by Isfahan-trained weavers.

PLATE 28

181

Karabagh

2,11m by 1,19m (6ft 11in. by 3ft 11in.) early nineteenth century

PLATE 29

The thick yarn used by the Karabagh and Kazak weavers lends a superficial similarity to the weave patterns of the two types. The weave pattern of the Karabagh does, however, display a consistent use of two weft shoots after every two rows of knots, and this is the main feature distinguishing it from the Kazaks. The symmetrical knot is used in both types but the conformation of the nodes is different. This design is known as the Chelaberd.

PLATE 30

183

Kashan

1,93m by 1,22m (6ft 4in. by 4ft) late nineteenth century

PLATE 31

The blue weft seen in this weave pattern is a very common but not an invariable feature of the Kashans. The distinguishing features are the shape of the nodes in combination with the appearance of the weft which is sometimes barely perceptible. A considerable depression of alternate warps, sometimes to the degree that the alternate warps are completely concealed behind their partners, is invariable. In this rug the node on the depressed warp is just visible.

PLATE 32

Kazak

2,08m by 1,07m (6ft 10in. by 3ft 6in.) nineteenth century

PLATE 33

The two main characteristics of the Kazak weave pattern are the use of the weft and the shape of the nodes. The weft shoots pass two, three, four or more times after each row of knots without apparent order. On a horizontal line the nodes of the symmetrical knots are longer than they are wide. In this rug the nodes are on an equal plane but this is not an invariable feature of the Kazaks, as some are found with a depression of alternate warps. This design is known as a Lambalo Kazak.

186

PLATE 34

Kerman

0,84m by 0,61m (2ft 9in. by 2ft) late nineteenth or early twentieth century

PLATE 35

This beautiful creation of the master-weaver Ali Kermani shows why the Kerman weavers were held in such high esteem throughout the rug weaving world. One warp is completely depressed and the visible nodes are contiguous with the visible nodes of the neighbouring knots. The fine weft is visible and of constant thickness. In all respects the weave pattern is refined in appearance.

PLATE 36

189

Khorasan

1,63m by 1,09m (5ft 4in. by 3ft 7in.) nineteenth century

PLATE 37

Alternate warps are depressed to the extent that only one node of each knot is visible. The weft passes twice between each two rows of knots but these weft lines are invisible. The most singular feature of the Khorasan weave pattern is the obvious path which traverses the whole width of the rug at regular intervals. This is created by four or more wefts passing after intervals of six or more rows of knots.

PLATE 38

Khotan

2,41m by 1,22m (7ft 11in. by 4ft) early nineteenth century

PLATE 39

We can find no basis for the assertion made by some authorities that there is a structural difference between the Kashgar and Khotan rugs. The weave pattern of this particular rug is finer and more compact than the average for the group and this may partly explain its survival. In general they are coarsely and loosely woven fabrics – a feature which does not support longevity. The appearance of the weft and a degree of depression of alternate warps, combined with rather large, fibrous knots are common features.

PLATE 40

193

Kirshehir

1,80m by 1,17m (5ft 11in. by 3ft 10in.) early nineteenth century

PLATE 41

The weft is red; the use of a red, orange or pink weft appears to be rapidly becoming a national as opposed to a regional custom in Turkey. The nodes of the symmetrical knots are on an even plane. The pattern constituted by the node shape and visible weft is very different in appearance from the other Turkish rugs illustrated in this book. Compare this with the weave patterns of the Ghiordes (Plate 21), Kula (Plate 45), Ladik (Plate 47), Melaz (Plate 49) and the Panderma (Plate 55).

194

PLATE 42

Kizil Ayak

2,90m by 2,24m (9ft 6in. by 7ft 4in.) second half nineteenth century

PLATE 43

At first glance the weave pattern of this rug is so similar to that of the Tekke (Plate 75) that these rugs could be regarded as variations of the same theme. However, this rug is an exceptionally fine Kizil Ayak whereas the Tekke weave is average for its group. The node shapes and their juxtaposition are common to both, as are the parallel vertical lines of the warp partners, but the main distinguishing feature between the two is the appearance of the weft.

196

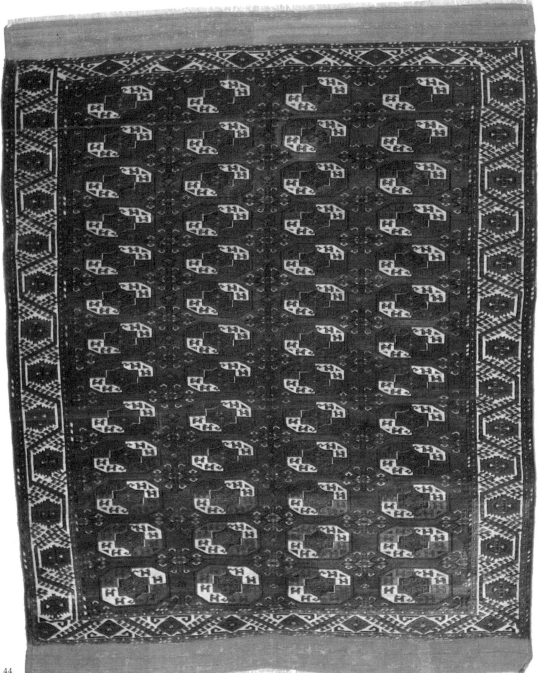

PLATE 44

197

Kula

1,58m by 1,35m (5ft 2in. by 4ft 5in.) nineteenth century

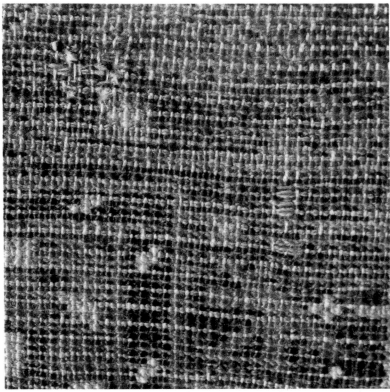

PLATE 45

Two distinct weft techniques are used. Firstly, there is the traverse of a weft across and back over alternate warps; then there is the use of two shoots each of which passes over and under the same warps. The effect of this latter technique is to expose the warp and lend the weave pattern an overall stringy appearance. A degree of depression of alternate warps is another characteristic feature of the Kula weave pattern.

198

PLATE 46

Ladik

1,75m by 1,07m (5ft 9in. by 3ft 6in.) late eighteenth century

PLATE 47

The appearance of the weft and the shapes of the adjacent nodes are the features which distinguish this weave pattern from that of the Ghiordes (Plate 21). The depression of the alternate warps is common to both.

200

PLATE 48

201

Melaz

1,37m by 1,04m (4ft 6in. by 3ft 5in.) nineteenth century

PLATE 49

The wefts are visible as fairly uniform lines and are used in regular succession – two wefts after every two rows of knots. The warps lie on an even plane and the nodes of the symmetrical knots are all the same shape.

202

PLATE 50

Nain

2,54m by 1,52m (8ft 4in. by 5ft) second half twentieth century

PLATE 51

One warp is completely hidden behind its partner and there is no gap between the visible nodes of neighbouring knots. The weft lines are barely perceptible. This very compact weave pattern has a knot density of approximately 500 to the square inch (7 750 to the square decimetre). A comparison with other Persian double-warped fabrics such as the Kerman (Plate 35) and the Kashan (Plate 31) will show that these three weave patterns are very dissimilar.

PLATE 52

205

Niriz

1,60m by 1,19m (5ft 3in. by 3ft 8in.) mid nineteenth century

PLATE 53

The left side of this weave pattern includes part of the selvedge to show the alternating colours which are a feature of these rugs. The shape of the knots and the almost concealed weft display an overall pattern which is completely different from the other rugs made in the Fars area, such as the Qashqa'i (Plate 57).

PLATE 54

Panderma

1,65m by 1,14m (5ft 5in. by 3ft 9in.) nineteenth century

PLATE 55

The ripple appearance of the weft is somewhat similar to the rugs of the eastern Caucasus and to those of Feraghan (Plate 19) but the shape of the nodes of the symmetrical knots is very different from both. The two nodes forming each knot are a different shape to one another. On the horizontal line one is conscious of the tram-line uniformity of the node pairs. There is an overall uniform appearance which is clearly different from that of the Ghiordes (Plate 21).

208

PLATE 56

209

Qashqa'i

2,67m by 1,40m (8ft 9in. by 4ft 7in.) second half nineteenth century

PLATE 57

Relative to the norm for Qashqa'i rugs, the weave pattern of this rug is exceptionally neat and uniform. A degree of depression of alternate warps is general. The combination of this feature, in conjunction with the node shape and the invariable use of a weft coloured in some shade of red, is the hallmark of the Qashqa'i rugs.

PLATE 58

211

Qum

2,06m by 1,45m (6ft 9in. by 4ft 9in.) twentieth century

PLATE 59

This weave pattern looks like a much coarser version of the modern Isfahan. The weave is coarser, the weft appears more frequently and the nodes are larger. These features are only apparent when complete rugs are compared side by side. It will be interesting to see if the Qum weave pattern matures into one more clearly distinguishable from that of the Isfahans.

PLATE 60

213

Salor

Fragment 0,61m by 0,31m (2ft by 1ft) possibly eighteenth century

PLATE 61

One warp is completely hidden behind its partner, a feature which we believe to be the norm in weaves of the Salor tribe of Turkestan. The nodes of the asymmetrical knots have a stringy appearance due to the loose ply of the pile threads – a feature not seen in the Saryk weaves. Another feature present in sections of all the Salor weaves examined by the authors is the barely visible extrusion of the thread of the concealed node, most clearly seen here in the central pink pattern. Wool and silk fragment: gift of Frank L. Loftus (acc. no. 08.376) by courtesy of Museum of Fine Arts, Boston.

214

PLATE 62

Sarouk (old)

1,52m by 1,09m (5ft by 3ft 7in.) mid nineteenth century

PLATE 63

Each weft line is visible along its complete traverse and varies in thickness. The variation is due to the irregular diameter of the weft threads. This feature, in combination with the appearance of the knots used to join the warp threads, is a characteristic of the old Sarouks. This weave pattern should be compared with the commercial Sarouk (Plate 65) and the Zel-i-Sultan (Plate 83).

216

PLATE 64

217

Sarouk (new)

1,98m by 1,12m (6ft 6in. by 3ft 8in.) twentieth century

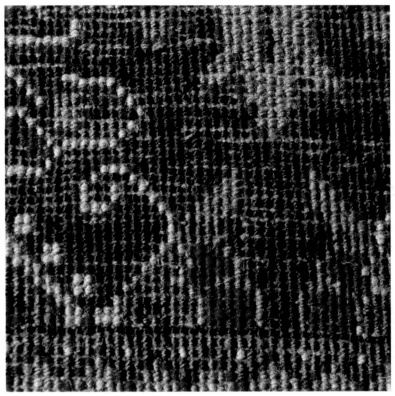

PLATE 65

The weft is generally blue though rugs with natural-coloured wefts are also found. More often than not the weft line is visible along its complete traverse. Alternate warps are completely depressed, and this feature can be detected by the appearance of a node in one colour where its neighbours on either side are different in colour. The shape and size of the nodes and the general appearance of the weave pattern is quite different from the old Sarouk (Plate 63).

218

PLATE 66

219

Saryk

1,88m by 1,52m with 25cm of kelim (6ft 2in. by 5ft with 10in. of kelim) mid nineteenth century

PLATE 67

The generation of Saryk weave patterns represented by this rug displays a pronounced corduroy-like appearance of the warp lines. In this particular rug one warp lies directly behind its partner. This is not an invariable feature though a degree of depression is common. A previous generation of Saryks, or possibly those from another area, have a different but clearly related weave pattern. Neither of these weave patterns can be confused with that of the Salor.

PLATE 68

Senneh

1,93m by 1,35m (6ft 4in. by 4ft 5in.) nineteenth century

PLATE 69

The most singular feature of this weave pattern is its granular appearance and feel. Contributing to this effect is the fine, tightly twisted yarn which is used for the knots. The warp lines are imperceptible. A single weft shoot is used but this is seldom visible along its complete traverse. The weft lines are rarely straight, more commonly wavy in appearance.

PLATE 70

223

Seyshour

2,11m by 1,30m (6ft 11in. by 4ft 3in.) mid nineteenth century

PLATE 71

In the weave pattern of this rug there is an obvious ridged appearance provided by the depression of alternate warps. The weft appearance is noteworthy as is the shape of the nodes, but these features are not invariable associates of the Seyshour design, nor are they invariable features of the rugs of the Kuba area. This point is enlarged upon in the dictionary and the monograph.

224

PLATE 72

225

Tabriz

2,06m by 1,30m (6ft 9in. by 4ft 3in.) late nineteenth century

PLATE 73

This generation of Tabriz rugs has a very different weave pattern from the later rugs such as those made by Taba Tabaie. In this one the weft appears in lines that are usually bowed and seldom visible along a complete traverse. The varying thickness of the weft thread is indicated by a widening of the weft where it is visible. Although the Isfahan (Plate 27) displays some features similar to the rugs of Tabriz, the two weave patterns are easily distinguishable.

PLATE 74

Tekke

2,46m by 1,83m (8ft 1in. by 6ft) early nineteenth century

PLATE 75

The neat parallel lines of warp pairs are a feature of this, the most common, Tekke weave pattern. We believe that the Tekke were the most skilled of the nomad weavers and supposedly learnt the craft from the Salor. If that is so the available evidence indicates that they excelled their teachers. This magnificent carpet has a weave which is average for the group. The difference between this weave pattern and that of the Kizil Ayak is discussed in the caption to the Kizil Ayak illustration.

228

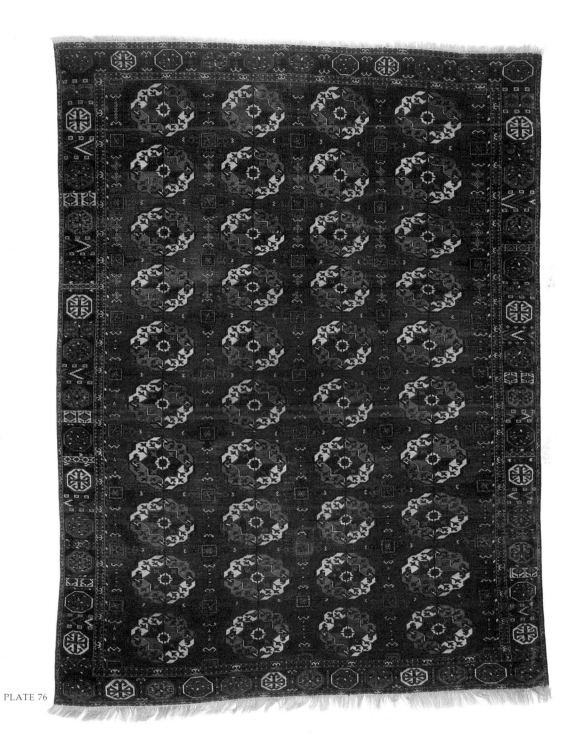

PLATE 76

229

Veramin

1,98m by 1,47m (6ft 6in. by 4ft 10in.) late nineteenth or early twentieth century

PLATE 77

One of the two nodes comprising each symmetrical knot is completely concealed behind its partner. The weft shoots are generally visible along the complete transverse line. The most important distinguishing feature of these manufactory Vera-mins is the pale blue weft which alternates with the use of an undyed weft. This feature is not present in the village or rural rugs which are sold under the same name.

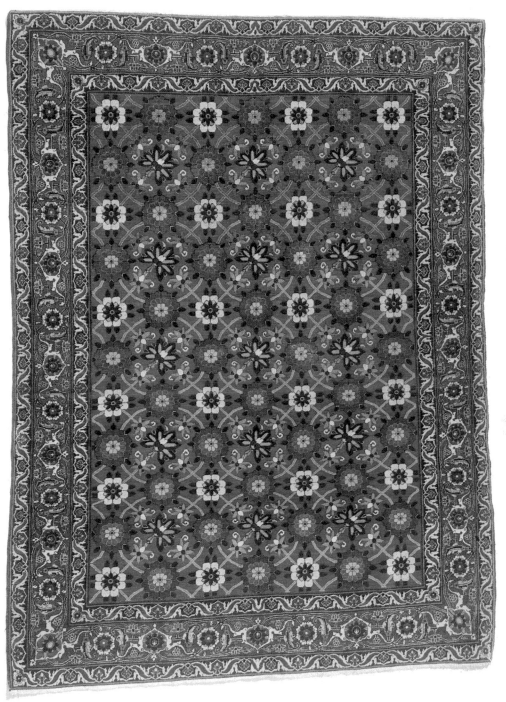

PLATE 78

Yürük

2,06m by 1,98m (6ft 9in. by 6ft 6in.) nineteenth century

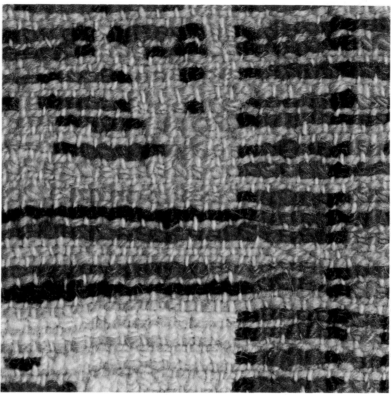

PLATE 81

An irregular succession of one to three very coarse weft shoots is used after every two rows of knots. Although succeeding weft shoots pass over and under different warps from the preceding shoot, the warps are nevertheless exposed where each shoot passes under a warp thread. This is a rare feature in Oriental rugs as more generally warps are only exposed when a single shoot is used between two rows of knots – as in the Hamadan (Plate 23). This rug is believed to be from the Konya area.

PLATE 82

235

Zel-i-Sultan

1,98m by 1,17m (6ft 6in. by 3ft 10in.) second half nineteenth century

PLATE 83

Although the visible nodes are contiguous with their neighbours, like the Kerman (Plate 35), the weft appearance in the two weave patterns is very different. There is a slight ripple in the weft line, not found in the Kerman, but appearing in a more pronounced way in the Feraghan (Plate 19). The conformation and uniformity of the Zel-i-Sultan nodes is, however, very different from those of the Feraghan. There is also some similarity with the old Sarouk (Plate 63), but the warp knots are not present in the Zel-i-Sultan nor is the varying thickness of the Sarouk weft line.

PLATE 84

237

Colour relief map ▶